Memories of United Counties
Part 2: Regional Reports

Memories of United Counties

Reminiscences of staff past and present
compiled by Caroline Cleaveley

Part 2: Regional Depots

Silver Link Publishing Ltd

First published in 2010

British Library Cataloguing in Publication Data

A catalogue record for this book is available from the British Library.

ISBN 978 1 85794 344 3

Silver Link Publishing Ltd
The Trundle
Ringstead Road
Great Addington
Kettering
Northants NN14 4BW

Tel/Fax: 01536 330588
email: sales@nostalgiacollection.com
Website: www.nostalgiacollection.com

Printed and bound in the Czech Republic

Author's note

In compiling this work, the present staff of Stagecoach East have asked for Bedford staff who died in the Second World War to be commemorated by reference to their Annual Busmen's Service. Kettering staff have also asked for tributes to be made to colleagues who lost their lives in service. This book is also a tribute to all staff who have passed away, leaving memories and photographs behind them.

If you worked for United Counties or Stagecoach East and have any additional information for this book, please contact me by telephone (01453 824810), email (caroline@cleaveley.wanadoo.co.uk), or post to 6 Glenthorne Close, Stonehouse, Glos GL12 6EF. Thank you for reading this book and I look forward to hearing from you; your information will be used to update the book if it is reprinted.

An Illustrated History of United Counties, a work in 17 volumes by Roger Warwick, is the ultimate history of the company from 1913 to 1999, and is available from Roger Warwick at 'Torestyn', 101 Broadway East, Northampton.

Acknowledgements

I would like to thank the management and staff of Stagecoach East (United Counties) and Arriva Shires and Essex; Roger Warwick, for his historical record of United Counties and his invaluable help with this publication; Steve Loveridge, for loan of archive material and help with identifying colleagues; *Kettering Evening Telegraph*; *Northampton Chronicle and Echo*; *Bus and Coach Preservation* magazine; *Bedford on Sunday* newspaper; and Kevin Lane, for his book on United Counties.

Roger Warwick MCIT

Steve Loveridge

Kettering Evening Telegraph

Contents

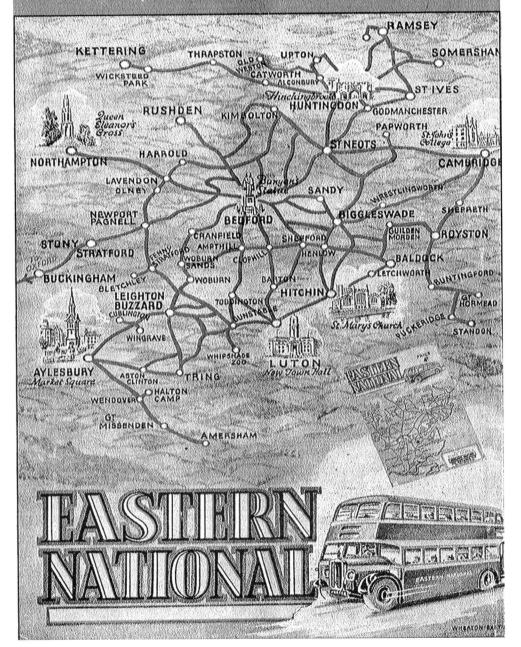

St Peter de Merton with St Cuthbert, Bedford

60TH ANNUAL BUSMEN'S SERVICE

Sunday 10th June 2007 at 3.15pm

1
Aylesbury

Aylesbury was the southernmost depot of United Counties and came into the company from Eastern National in 1952.

Leonard Gentle

Mrs Birch has supplied the following information about her father. He first worked for Chater Lea Manufacturing Co Ltd in Icknield Way Letchworth, from January 1930 to July 1933. He

Mrs Birch with her father, Leonard Gentle, and John Tate at Mr Gentle's retirement dinner. In the background is his prized power wood saw. *Mrs Birch collection*

then worked for London Transport (Green Line) in a clerical role from July to October 1933. He was made redundant and, after a week's unemployment, joined Eastern National Omnibus Company in Luton. During the Second World War he served in the Army Medical Corps as a dental technician, returning to the bus industry on demob.

In 1948 Leonard attained his RSA qualifications in Road Transport Operation (Passenger), elements of Road Transport Engineering and Accounts & Statistics. When United Counties took over Luton Area, Leonard transferred with them. After working at Hitchin, Aylesbury and Luton, he retired as superintendent at Kettering (see Chapter 11) in April 1981. He had medals awarded for 25, 40 and 45 years' service. In total he worked for the company for 47 years.

The first company house that the family lived in was at Aston Clinton near Aylesbury. It was cold and full of dry rot, and when the fire was lit the whole house would become smoky. The house's main claim to fame was that the previous owner had drowned herself in the water butt.

United Counties sold this house soon after the Gentles moved in, and they were transferred to a newly purchased property in Bedgrove, Aylesbury. While at Aylesbury Leonard could not drive and had to be taxied around the area by his son-in-law. One day he was sent to Wingrave to an accident where a single-decker had knocked down a pole and ended up in a ditch.

People remembered at Aylesbury were the Secretary, Mrs Berkeley, and one of the Inspectors, Mr Buckmaster. Leonard did eventually learn to drive, in a Ford Anglia.

George Hawkins

Aylesbury ran 16 buses and employed about 50 staff. George found it strange, as there was no canteen and only a small mess room. The only joint service was to Amersham with London Transport. However, this soon lapsed as the bus was needed elsewhere, and eventually London Transport stopped the service altogether.

At Aylesbury, conductress Dot Fitton was well-liked. She used to carry a bag of sweets with her and would rather spend time feeding the driver and passengers than get the bus out on time! Fortunately

Long service awards at Aylesbury, 8 March 1963, including Len and Stan Frost, Bill Lawrence, A. Simonds, P. Jeffery, F. Mortimer, T. Norgate, W. Stainton and R. Swan. Leonard Gentle is sixth from the left, with J. Robinson on his right. *Bucks Advertiser, Mrs Birch collection*

the drivers only had her for one week a year and had to tolerate her ways. If they were running late she said it was the driver's responsibility, not hers. Dot also did not want to give anyone change; passengers without the correct fare would wait for the next bus if they saw Dot coming. At the end of the day she would have the heaviest bag of change (three to four times heavier) and would be struggling to carry it!

Driver Wallace Chumer had to use a rubber ring to sit on, and was teased as a result. Eva Pantling, another conductress, used to chatter all the time. Len and Stan Frost both worked on the buses. Mr Swan was the depot engineer and Mr Sell the Chief Engineer (Head Office). George also remembers Bill Lawrence.

David Shadbolt

David was born in Northamptonshire and educated in Essex before he became a Senior Management trainee at Yorkshire Traction from 1979 to 1981. He began his involvement with United Counties in 1981, when he was employed as Depot Superintendent at Aylesbury. This was a small depot and a good training ground for a young manager. From those early days at Aylesbury, David remembers Inspectors Bill

Smith, Bert Stone and Harry Blencoe, together with depot engineer Norman Moore and area engineer Paul Woolmore, who now works in Harlow. He also remembers many of the drivers, some of whom are still working in Aylesbury today.

Malcolm Wearn

Malcolm tried many jobs on leaving school. He spent some time working on farms, serving in the forces and working in a bakery before settling for United Counties buses. Starting as a driver in 1972, he graduated to driving the coaches and worked the National Express routes with the private hires. He also drove on the X15 services to Milton Keynes.

In 1992 he became the In Service Driver Trainer, later becoming an Instructor and an Inspector in 1993. At present he is the main Instructor for Arriva Shires and still works out of Aylesbury. With colleagues Dennis Mulligan and Arthur Rose, he is a relief controller at Victoria Coach Station.

Malcolm Wearn and Inspector Tom Hawkins. *NBC News*

2
Bedford

Bedford was the main depot for that county, and had sub-depots at Biggleswade and Huntingdon.

Top: **St Peters Bus Station in Bedford.**
Roger Warwick collection

Above left: **Bedford St Johns Depot, showing the Depot Manager's house.**
Roger Warwick collection

Above right: **Mr Ernie Howe, a Bedford busman from 1928 to 1968, at St Peters Bus Station.** *Dick Watson collection*

Left: **Some of the driving and conducting team at St Peters. Standing at the back are Freddie Stroud and Norman Pedler, while the front row includes Jessie Layton, Esther McGowan, Peggy Woods, Ernie Howe and Ms Batchelor.** *Dick Watson collection*

Arthur Ford

Arthur Ford sadly died as this book was being prepared and, so his memories will be from others, including his brother Roy.

Arthur went to work in Nottingham when he left home, then on his return he joined the bus company as a conductor. He rose to become a bus driver, coach driver and later an Inspector. He appears in this role in Kevin Lane's book on United Counties, *Glory Days*.

When driving, his main conductor was one Mike Mahoney, and in retirement he used to go out on many trips with his friend Gordon. Although officially retired, Arthur worked part-time for United Counties and Stagecoach, doing various tasks until he had to give up at the age of 80. Three of these tasks involved office work, loading cases on coaches and piloting new drivers round the various routes.

Living opposite Bedford Bus Station, he became the unofficial caretaker and only lived for the buses. He remembered this time more vividly than anything else.

Roy Ford

Roy joined United Counties in 1953 just after the Eastern National takeover. He worked out of the old St Peters Bus Station, and when he left the new bus station was still a dream.

Both Roy's parents had worked on the buses; his mother was a cleaner and his father a battery fitter. His brother Arthur also worked for the company most of his working life, when he returned from Nottingham, until he was 80 years old (see above). His brother-in-law, James Leadbetter, also worked for the company.

Top: **James Rolfe from Bedford, who looks after the bus stops in Bedfordshire.** *Stagecoach Bedford collection*

Above: **St Peters used to be crowded with buses and customers.** *Roger Warwick collection*

In the 1950s, if your family worked for a company and had a good record, you were very likely to get a job. Roy was working for the General Post Office in Bedford and went to work at United Counties because the pay was better. When he started he was paid 14s 2d a week, and when he left in 1960 his pay had risen to £3 per week. All staff had to join the union before they were allowed to work for the company.

Roy found that driving Bristol buses was not too bad, but the Leyland double-deckers were heavy on the steering. He particularly

Top right: **Arthur Ford (sitting, extreme left) at a long service award ceremony in 1978. Others present are (back row) Richard Dunkley, Alan Buttiphant, Tony Cassidy and Frederick Pack, and (front row) Roy Burdett, Irwin Dalton, Peter Spittles and Colin Clubb.** *Colin Clubb collection*

Above: **Arthur hard at work in Bedford Bus Station.** *John Aldridge*

he could be working up to 18 hours a day and the pay rate covered the whole time.

In the 1950s Roy remembers that most staff walked, cycled or caught a bus to work. The Superintendent had the quickest journey, as he lived in the company house next door to the garage.

The top speed on coaches was 48mph and when on any service it was a case of getting going and putting the accelerator to the floor to keep to the schedule. Roy remembers that the coaches also did private hire work; on one occasion three drivers and two coaches went down to the South Coast. Drivers took it in turns to drive and rest. He remembers that two shifts were worked, one from 5.00am till 2.00pm and the second from 2.00pm to midnight.

Roy remembers that the company had sub-depots at Clophill and St Neots. Clophill had two vehicles, one crewed by a driver, Bill Juffs, and Florrie Lloyd, a conductress; these two always worked together. The garage was a shed next door to the Flying Horse, the village pub. Another bus was crewed by Jim Shelton and a Miss or Mrs Stevens. Roy remembers that buses from Bedford to Luton were exclusively run from Bedford. One evening trip entailed taking passengers to Luton and running light (empty) back to Clophill. After putting the bus to bed the crew then waited to catch the following Luton to Bedford bus. One day they decided to walk until the bus caught them up. Clophill had a very scary forest, which in more recent times was the site of a murder,

remembers a single-decker with an engine out the front, like a Bedford OB, which was known as 'the Pig'. In the 1950s Roy remembers that he had to drive 3 hours on local services, then drive to Oxford for a change. One lonely trip was the 10.15pm to Cranfield, which set off back to Bedford at about 11.00pm; by the time he arrived back and put the bus to bed at the garage, it was about midnight.

Roy had regular conductors on his buses and only had others when he worked overtime. He also said that overtime could be paid on a 'spreadover' rate, as

Bedford's All Hallows Bus Station, where Arthur Ford spent much of his career. *Roger Warwick collection*

and Roy was glad when the next bus arrived.

Three Jacksons worked for the Bedford area. One used to deal with the football pools and the other two were brothers who worked at St Neots. Roy is not sure but he thinks that the St Neots buses were parked somewhere in Blunham.

In the 1950s the conductors were each responsible for reconciling their own money at the end of the day. Even at midnight they had to make sure that all tallied before they went home. If a penny was missing the Inspector would make them find out where it had gone. In more modern times the drivers bag up their money and give it to Dave Melen, who sorts it out for them.

Roy played for the company cricket team, which consisted of mainly Northampton and Bedford staff. The teams played against seemed to be from other Tilling Group companies. Roy remembers a trip to Chesterfield, where he was allowed to drive the coach for part of the trip. As he drove so well, he was invited to drive coaches on a regular basis.

Roy remembers that the company had a rota system for Christmas, and staff were allowed only one

day for the holiday. He had only just reached having Boxing Day off when he left the company and went to work for Texas Instruments.

After he left, Roy and his wife attended many Social Club events and he particularly remembers a trip to Duxford Museum and bus rally.

Andrew Pike

Andrew is now the Assistant Manager at Kettering, but he started his career with East Kent at Ramsgate, being a crew driver in 1971. He then became a driver of one-man-operated (OMO) buses, as it paid 50p more per week. He then went on to the coaching and private hire work, where one of his duties was Margate to London Victoria Coach Station.

Three years later he changed employers and went to work for Neils Coaches (later Capital Coaches) at Heathrow. This work involved much tourist and continental work.

After three years he decided to change jobs again, and this time he went to work for United Counties at Biggleswade, then Bedford in 1978, staying there until 1987.

The latter year saw the break-up of United Counties, and the bus wars in Bedford began. Andrew started a bus company and called it LAP travel. He

Children's Christmas parties were held for many years in the Corn Exchange, Bedford, and Father Christmases included Arthur Ford, Sid Goodwin and Stan Burton. About 500 people were catered for, including children from Barnardo's and Kempston Lodge. *Dick Watson collection*

Father Christmases Stan Burton and Arthur Ford at Bedford. *Dick Watson collection*

started services to Oakley in competition with Ray Ramsey at Bedford United Counties; he felt he had won the competition when his vehicles developed problems. He had three Leyland/DAF mini-coaches, which broke down every 35,000 miles when the engine blew. This apparently was due to short dipsticks and too much oil in the engine. The cost of these repairs was too much and the company folded.

Andrew then went back to Bedford and was taken on again, as a driver, working until 1999, which was when Stagecoach changed its name and did away with United Counties. Andrew was the Chairman of the Bedford union and enjoyed that post.

In 2006 the deputy's post at Kettering was advertised, and he moved to get the job.

Andrew remembers many faces of his former colleagues at Bedford and Biggleswade but not their names. However, he does remember Arthur Ford, Dick and Derek Watson and Dragoljub Kalicann, who was nicknamed 'Mr Tito' after the Yugoslav dictator, because he looked like him. He also remembers well the Travel Shop staff, particularly Jeanette and John.

Clive Jones

Clive started work at Bedford as a Schedules Clerk in July 1974. He was taught to do his job by David Harris, who was a very meticulous worker. He had to report to Jack Hartley, Assistant Traffic Manager (Administration), at Northampton on his first day, and spent half a day each with Allan Crabbe, Ray Ramsey and Bob Whiteley. Clive seemed to do the Schedule B work. At wages time all staff lent a hand to stuff the envelopes. Occasionally he had to check the bus mileages daily, and work on the switchboard when required.

Clive worked with Steve Loveridge in Schedules, and also remembers Frances Piercey in the Waybill Office at Bedford Road, Northampton. One day he was sent to check some waybills in her office; she ruled the office with a rod of iron and sat at her desk at one end glowering down at her staff checking the waybills. The Chief Clerk at Bedford was Richard Askew (still in the same office in 2007). One part of his job was to time the routes, and he spent time in 1978 timing the 402 route from Wellingborough to

the Co-op Laundry in Irthlingborough. He also timed buses in the Corby area. While doing these jobs he was working for Ray Ramsey, the Depot Supervisor at Kettering. He also had a brief stint at Stony Stratford

The working bays and bus storage area inside Bedford Depot. *Roger Warwick collection*

Fitters working on the 'swimming pool' bays at Bedford Depot. *Roger Warwick collection*

before returning to Bedford.

The Bedford office rarely received a visit from the General Manager. When he did come, the place was painted and all road staff had to wear their best uniforms. Like the Army, even the coal was painted! He also remembers that one manager (John Birks) wrote a detailed volume on the National Bus Company.

Clive was told that the only former Eastern National staff at Bedford Road were Bob Coote, who was also at Wellingborough for some time, and Percy Greaves. All staff from Bedford, Biggleswade, Hitchin and Luton also transferred. When United Counties was split into the Eastern and Western areas, each area was a self-contained unit and the staff did not mix often at junior level.

Clive left United Counties in 1980 and worked for Darlington Transport as Traffic Assistant and Operations Manager (1980-86), the Port Elizabeth Tramway and Algo Bus Company (1986-95), and for Seychelles Public Corporation as Traffic Manager (1996-99). In 2000 he returned to the UK and spent six months at the Oxford Bus Company, then moved to Rugby with Midland Red South (Stagecoach). He is now the Commercial Manager for the latter Company and in January 2007 was joined by Ray Ramsey again, but this time as Ray's boss.

David Battle

David started his career with Eastern National in 1949 at Bedford Depot on the running shift, and worked there for 2½ years This was unskilled work and involved breakdowns and general maintenance work in the depot. He left for a year before United Counties started, but returned when Mr Stocker, Works Foreman, asked him to come back as a skilled worker in 1952. David worked there until his retirement in 1993.

Other departments were controlled by chargehands, who were skilled workers. David remembers that the Dock Chargehand covered the pit area, and he himself worked in that role in United Counties days. One of his main colleagues was Bob Bartrum, and they worked closely together. He remembers especially when Johnny Johnson was the Depot Engineer, and lived in the house attached to the depot.

He remembers that one recovery truck was an AEC Matador, converted for that use; it was a good vehicle and could lift anything. Apparently the Supervisor at the time thought that it needed replacing and bought Ford vehicles; that at Bedford had to be lengthened and had a lifting apparatus attached, which was supposed to lift 5 tons, but when it went to MOT for certifying they would only pass it for 35cwt. This was useless and it was used for the rest of its stay as a towing vehicle only. Recovery trucks were under the HGV2 category of vehicles and required the relevant licence to drive them. The area covered by the recovery trucks was from Scratchwood Services to Watford Gap Services on the M1, and the A5 before that; the A1 was also covered.

One day the running team was sent out to the A1 at Sandy to collect a Bristol RE that belonged to Lincolnshire Road Car. One of the rear tyres had caught fire, setting fire to the rest of the bus. Fortunately no one was injured. By the time the breakdown truck arrived, all they had to tow was a bent chassis with a pile of twisted metal lying on top. This was covered over and dumped at the back of the depot until Lincolnshire decided what to do with it.

All the tyres, for buses and lorries, where supplied by Goodyear, which also supplied the fitters. His favourite gearbox was built by Wilson, as it was the easiest for the fitter.

David attended many courses during his career. Most he felt were useless to him, but one he did find worthwhile was the brake course at Vauxhall in Luton; the information gained was used all the time.

David passed his driving test and used to go out on service on a Saturday afternoon when required, mainly at holiday time. He did shift work; the hours were 5.00am-3.00pm and 3.00pm-midnight. Sometimes the hours would be longer if he attended a breakdown. In later years the start time on the early shift was 6.00am.

David recalls that the Stagecoach format and livery was designed locally in Biggleswade.

John Kelly

John was a driver and in the early days buses used Silver Street, Bedford, in both directions. With restrictive clearances, both buses had to be as close to the kerb as possible. One day his conductor began ringing the bell like a mad

thing. John did not realise that anything was wrong, but apparently a woman had been carrying a brand-new typewriter down the footpath and the carriage must have hit the mudguard as the bus passed. This had the result of knocking the typewriter out of her hands and it went under the wheels of the bus. The road behind was strewn with the debris and there were keys everywhere. The company had to pay for a new typewriter and John did not live it down for a while.

However, this was not the only incident of this kind, as on another occasion a pedestrian claimed that a bus had knocked her new teapot or kettle out of her hand and broken the tip off the end. The bus company could not have her going without her tea, so bought her a new one.

Alan Parfitt

One of Alan's memories of Bedford was the day that Kenneth Wellman was admonished by Superintendent Maurice Jewitt for putting a Bristol FLF on the town service 101. This vehicle was replaced urgently and put on a country service. Sometimes Bedford buses had running numbers to show which rota the bus

Bedford's training bus has an outing to Kettering in March 1989 with one of the spare Routemasters. This vehicle is now owned by Brian Souter, Chief Executive of the Stagecoach Group. *Author's collection*

was working. Bristol FLFs were not allowed on the town services; only when service 103 later went OMO with Bristol VRs were buses larger that 60-seaters used.

John Potter

John was born in Aberdeen and moved to Clapham, near Bedford, at the age of four. His father taught at a school in Sandy, hence the reason for coming to Bedford. At the age of nine the family moved into the centre of Bedford, near the bus station. John remembers that buses used to pass his house daily. He used to go to school in Clapham, then in Sandy on the Biggleswade route. The buses were mainly R-registration Volvo Olympians with a few of the old Bristol VRs.

At 16, John needed to do work experience for two weeks, so naturally he went to Bedford Depot. Working there in 1998 he remembers John Bass, the Engineering Manager, Paul Brimley, Brian Flute and Tony in the Body Shop, and Paint Shop staff Mick Hill, Tony Evangelista and Garry. The only fitter he can remember was called Andy. Other people he remembers from his Bedford times are Ray Ramsey, Richard Askew, John Robertson and Lyn Worboys.

This work experience gave John a good insight into bus management. He subsequently went to college in Bedford and Gloucester, then started in the bus industry. His first job was with First Bus in South Yorkshire, then he moved back to Gloucester after a year and now drives for Stagecoach in Stroud.

Favourite buses included Olympian 603, which came to an untimely end in the side of a house, having been blown over in the wind. His favourite Bristol VR was 937, and he can remember the over-all adverts on buses, especially the one for Jockey Y-fronts.

He is interested in the L-reg Dennis Darts and Olympians. He is also a keen photographer and has photographed many of the buses at Bedford and Kettering. He is now active in the Stroud preservation movement, and meets up with his friends from Bedford annually at the Showbus event in Duxford, Cambridgeshire.

Bedford Routemaster 703 on the 101 route. *Mr A. Askew*

Mick Johnson

Mick has driven for Stagecoach at Bedford for 18 years, and recalls two amusing incidents. The first was after a bad snowstorm when he was out at Souldrop. A JCB had cleared the road to just the width of two cars, so no car could pass a bus. A Nissan Micra was coming the other way and tried to pass Mick, but became stuck. As there were no passengers on board, Mick left the bus and offered to lift and push the car out of the snow. This proved to be tricky as the back wheels were spinning and the car was going nowhere. The car driver then had a brainwave. 'If I get out and push as well we can get the car out!' He then remembered that he was actually driving at the time, so stayed where he was.

The second incident occurred in Midland Road, Bedford, just after it was made into a one-way street. Mick was driving a Leyland-engined bus that day, which at that time were very quiet. Seeing a couple of police officers walking away from him in the middle of the road, he crept up behind them unheard. The police were confused by the reactions of passers-by who were shouting, 'Look behind you!' Thinking they were being jeered at, they ignored it and carried on unaware of Mick and his bus behind them. The next bit was like a couple in a horror movie looking round and seeing the monster behind them. Mick could not stop laughing for the rest of the day.

Jagire Singh

Jagire was a driver at Bedford and learned to drive on the 'Yellow Peril', Bristol FS KBD 714D. His most enjoyable time was driving the Routemasters on route 101. This service ran at 10-minute intervals with 10 minutes at the turnaround, but if the conductor was good at his job they had a 15-minute rest. His favourite bus Routemaster 705. He now works in the Travel Shop at Bedford Bus Station.

His children, as reminded by their mother, used to enjoy pulling the string to stop Daddy driving the bus!

Dick and Derek Watson

Dick Watson Senior used to work for a Mr Franklin, who operated his own coach service near Bedford. Dick remembers that there were two horses; one was used most times and the other was for climbing extra-steep hills at Carlton – the spare horse was walked separately.

Dick and Derek Watson both worked for United Counties/Stagecoach, and both retired at the same time. Dick joined in July 1954 and worked at Bedford as a conductor, driver, coach-driver then Inspector for 25 years; the pay increase from driver to inspector was only about a £1 a week. On official retirement after 45 years, in 1999, Derek worked part-time on school runs. During his time at United Counties and Stagecoach East, he was Secretary of the Social Club for 30-odd years, and at the time of writing Dick is the President of the Social Club. During his time he has amassed many photographs and other items of memorabilia concerning the buses, and provided about 200 items of paper and photographs for this work.

When Stagecoach used a mobile booking office, Dick used to man it for three days a week, while John Robertson manned it on other days. Dick used to go to St Neots, among other places.

Colleagues he remembers include Inspector Percy Warboys, whose son Derrick worked for the company as a fitter in Kettering. He also remembers Joe Wallis

at Rushden Garage and Johnny Johnson, who was the Depot Engineer at Bedford. Mr Jewitt was the Superintendent at Bedford at this time. Sam Allison was also at Bedford Depot, before Dick himself. He also remembers Stan Burton, who was a good mate; he was a driver, and later an Inspector, at Bedford. Mr Cornwall was the Secretary and Treasurer of one of the clubs well into his 80s.

Dick remembers the old bus station at Bedford St Peters. He recalls that any spare buses had to be parked on Foster Hill Road, to the annoyance of the residents, and called back to the bus station when required. He always goes to the Annual Busmen's Service at St Peter's Church, and sometimes takes boards with his collection of old photographs. Dave Deacy tells us that the service, first held in 1947, was initially designed to commemorate six Eastern National busmen who were killed in the First World War, but the bus men and women now remember all their fallen colleagues in all wars; United Counties also lost staff. A plaque with their names is in St Peter's Church, Bedford, and also in the Travel Shop at Bedford. After each service a dinner, arranged by the Retired Bus People's Committee, is held for retired and present staff; the first was held in 1962.

Buses Dick remembers include Bristol RELH ABD 251B, which he took on a trip to Margate. Another bus he remembers is Bristol LS JBD 986, in which on a trip to Hastings he was stopped for speeding at between 30 and 40 miles per hour.

One Christmas a tobacconist gave the busmen a large quantity of cigarettes, and this started off the fund for retired busmen. The cigarettes were raffled

Bedfordshire on Sunday, May 30, 1999

Long service: Drivers park after 87 years at wheel

Bus brothers bid a fond fare-well

TWO brothers who between them have clocked up 87 years on the buses have retired within days of each other.

Bedford's first bus company was set up by their great grandfather Robert Franklin with a horse and cart in the early part of the century.

The business has since changed hands many times and is now part of Stagecoach, for whom Dick and Derek Watson worked as drivers.

Dick, 65, said "If we'd been paid a pound for every mile we've travelled we'd be millionaires by now.

History

I think 45 years is long enough but I will miss the place and the people."

Derek, 63, said: "We've seen a lot of changes."

The brothers have played an important part in the history of Bedford bus station.

They were the last men to work at the old St Peter's Depot before it closed and Derek still has his first uniform.

Stagecoach is no stranger to long serving employees. Inspector Davis Coles retired recently after 42 years and depot traffic manager Ray Ramsey is still going strong after 36 years.

As a special surprise on Saturday, Dick's wife arranged for a vintage bus to pick her husband up on his final day.

■ **Off the buses:** Dick (left) and Derek (right), neither brother stops working for years, then two retire at once as it was too much of a problem to distribute them fairly. Dick was on the committee of this organisation for many years, and is still a member.

Dick remembers that the first United Counties lady driver, Miss Georgina Hill, who was employed at Biggleswade in the 1970s.

Dick's wife worked at Bedford as a conductress, only leaving when she had to look after their children. She returned to being a conductress afterwards and retired with the other conductors/resses in the 1970s. Their daughter now drives a Park and Ride bus in Cambridge.

Ray Ramsey

Ray left school in 1963 and started work at Bedford under Area Manager Maurice Jewitt. He never attended an interview, but was asked to join the company by Ken Wellman.

Ray had been friends with Richard Askew since the age of 11 and both joined the company together,

Ken Jackson (left) and Dick Watson with their wives at a social gathering. *Dick Watson collection*

one in Bedford and one in Northampton. However, both were bored after a few months and swapped jobs, Ray going to Northampton and Richard to Bedford.

Ray's job was part schedules and part licences with Bob Coote; he worked with Ralph Arnold (Scheduler West area). In 1967 the schedules were decentralised and Ray was moved to Luton, where he worked with Bob Rumbold, the bowler-hatted boss, and Dave Tasker. In March 1969 Ray became bored again and applied for a conducting job at Rushden, which was the nearest vacancy to his home in Irthlingborough. He did not actually do the job, however, as he was requested by Tom White to help with the next fares increase.

In 1970 Ray became the Fares & Licensing Officer at Bedford Road, Northampton, then Depot Supervisor at Kettering from 1975 to 1987; his job title was changed to Superintendent Kettering Area, which included Wellingborough and Corby.

At Kettering, Ray became the chauffeur for Leonard Gentle, collecting him by company car in the morning and taking him home in the evening. Ray also had lunch at home, as he took Leonard home for his lunch.

In 1987, with the sale to Stagecoach, Ray took up the same job in the larger area of Bedford, working with new Managing Director, Barry Hinckley, who came from Cumberland Motors.

In 2000 Ray took over as Commercial Manager, after acting in the role for 18 months. When Inglis Lyon took over as Managing Director, Ray transferred

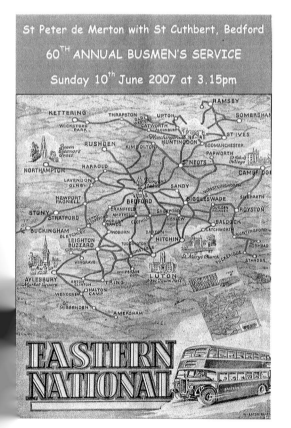

The programme from the 60th Annual Busmen's Service in 2007. *Dick Watson collection*

Top and above: **Retired Bedford members and friends in 1962.** *Dick Watson collection*

back to Bedford again as Tenders & Contracts Manager. He made Bedford a very profitable cost centre over the next few years. In the meantime, United Counties merged with Cambus and became Stagecoach East.

Ray's final move was back to Northampton in 2003, dealing with contracts again. At the time of writing he is now the Commercial Analyst for Midland Red South at Rugby. He started there in January 2007, after working for United Counties and Stagecoach East for 43 years.

Staff that Ray remembers are Dennis Mulligan,

Driver Les Bayes and Ray Ramsey inaugurate a new service to London. *Kettering Evening Telegraph*

Arthur Rose and Garry Seamarks from Luton and Dunstable. He also knew Des Banyard, who became company driver for Brian Souter when he retired as a bus driver. Other staff he remembers are Stan Simons; George Hawkins and Richard Christian, who left to run their own bus company; Terry Mead, who worked at Huntingdon; James Rolfe, Curly Rolf's nephew; and Barry Hinde at Huntingdon, who had very good handwriting and became the Internal Auditor, then Manager, at Huntingdon. At Bedford, Ray remembers Tom Watt, who was a Morris Minor enthusiast, and Dragoljub Kalicann, who was nicknamed 'Mr Tito' (because he looked like him); Dragoljub retired in 1977 and joined the retired members club. Jim Burley was another long-serving staff member, starting as a parcels boy at 14; Peter Brown also started early, at the age of 15. Ray also remembers Yvonne Taylor at Luton. Finally, at

L. Waller with Jim Burley (celebrating 50 years of service with Eastern National and United Counties at Bedford), D. G. F. Rawlinson and Colin Clubb at the annual awards in 1975. *Northampton Chronicle & Echo, Colin Clubb collection*

Northampton, 'Tich' Haws was at the Works, having started his career at Irthlingborough Body Shop and Works before Bedford Road was built.

Dragoljub Kalicann with a colleague on one of
the retired bus people's trips. *Dick Watson collection*

The Bedford Sports & Social Club BBQ

Organised at the Meltis Club by a group of Bedford
employees led by Vince Valandra, this annual event
gives the bus people and their families a chance to
relax and raise money for local charities.

The main team game was a form of volleyball,
while individuals were catered for with a novel game
consisting of throwing a toilet roll, in its sleeve, as far
as you can using a throwing device similar to a broom
handle with a stop (to hold the toilet roll) about 5
inches from the hand end. Competitions were for
men, women and children of different ages.

For children the organisers supplied a roundabout
and face painting, while the adults enjoyed the
drinking facility of the club and the barbecue itself.

Hair today, gone tomorrow

A BEDFORD bus driver made a bald statement in favour
of a very worthy cause.

Sid Lovett (64) shaved off his hair to raise £3000 for
Keech Cottage Children's Hospice in Streatley near Luton.

Sid – who has worked for Stagecoach Bedford for 37
years and retires in November – was inspired by a TV show
in which young children helped raise money for their local
hospice.

"I looked in the mirror one morning and decided that
my way of raising money would be to shave off my long
locks and ask my colleagues at work to sponsor me," said
Sid who, although bald on top, used to have flowing hair all
around.

"I had an enthusiastic response from drivers, staff and
managers."

Sid raised £1500, which was matched by Stagecoach to
make the impressive total of £3000.

The long and the short of it: Hospice
fundraiser Sid Lovett (right) with, from
left: Vince Valandra and Dave Davis from
Stagecoach Bedford and Nicki Rowley
from Keech Cottage.

Sid Lovett has worked for Bedford for 37 years, and this article from *On Stage*,
the company paper, describes his fundraising successes.

From the Bedford Archive
All photographs from the Dick Watson collection.

Dick Cleavey and Stan Burton

Alec Field and Ken Jackson

Alec Field, Cyril Rothwell and Peter Brown

**Bill
Doughty**

Madge Beavers and Cyril Shaw

Peter Rainer, George Dashwood and friends

Mrs Abele, Peggy and Arthur Woods

Stan Grantham and friends

Madge Lawrence and friend

John Broughton and friends

Les Bidewell

Brian McCall (seated left) and colleagues

Fitter Mr Sharpe

Jeff Ingram and Tom Watts

The 1962 football team

Ernie Howe and friend

Visits from Father Christmas, including Dave Coles, Frank Jones, John Benstead and John Tysoe.

3
Biggleswade

The Half Moon public house: Biggleswade Depot was to the rear, with its entrance to the left. The building on the right is the new offices. *Roger Warwick collection*

Biggleswade depot after being doubled in size.
Roger Warwick collection

Biggleswade Depot was a sub-depot of Bedford, and was originally a smaller building behind the ancient Half Moon public house.

Mick Arnold

Mick started work as a conductor with Birch Bros at their Henlow Camp depot in 1963, and also did office work. He had gone to school on Birch buses, and remembers the Leyland double-deckers especially. He remembers Stan Knight from those days. Graham Smith from Luton wrote a book about Birch Bros and Mick appeared in various bus photographs.

In 1968 the Henlow garage closed and most of the staff moved to United Counties. In Mick's case he moved to Biggleswade, while his friend Mick Griffin moved to Rushden. Mick managed to attach himself to an older driver at Biggleswade, who was a pleasure to work with, and Mick and he became close family friends. Fred Rook went out and showed him the routes on which he would be working.

Mick was a crew driver and later a One Person Operation driver. His first conductress was Georgina Hill, who went on to be the first lady driver in service with United Counties at Biggleswade. Mick was sent to Northampton for his driving test with Norman Redhead; he had a Bristol Lodekka for his test, and afterwards Arthur Woods took him on his first night driving. The KSW only had one dipped headlight, as the other one went out. This was very disconcerting, as it was difficult to see where he was going.

Bert Gray was the Inspector at Biggleswade and worked for the

A group on a trip with (extreme right) Bill Smith Snr and Fred Kitchener. *Mick Arnold collection*

Another trip, Messrs Batson, Whitfield and Spinks. *Mick Arnold collection*

company for more than 40 years. The office clerk for many years was Sylvia Askew; her husband Richard was in charge of the clerical department at Bedford, and at the time of writing is still working there. Fred Rook was the senior conductor at Biggleswade, and had gone to school with Mick's mother; he was nicknamed 'Sarah', while Mick's nickname was 'Daisy'. The fitters seemed to live at Moggerhanger.

Other staff that Mick remembers are driver Fred Kitchener; Rodney Albone, who also ran a shop in Biggleswade; driver Bill Gravestock; and Harold Mays. Kit and Frank Wilkins were the outstation crew at Arrington Bridge, Derek Hallibone was a driver, and Mrs Abele used to knit all the time when she was not conducting. Inspector Whitmore was at Bedford, as was driver Jeff Ingram.

Richard and Bill Smith Jnr were keen railway enthusiasts and used to arrange trips to different parts of the country using United Counties vehicles. Mick remembers that a trip was arranged to Sheringham in Norfolk one Sunday and Bristol VR 757 was used to Huntingdon. It was then locked in the depot and one of Huntingdon's own buses used instead; 757 was

collected on the way home. Bus preservationist John Robertson owns three Bristol VR buses, including Biggleswade's 757 and Bristol RELL 319.

Mick was an active trade unionist and was the Area Officer of the TGWU in Biggleswade for 14 years, although the branch was not as vocal as that at Bedford. He remembers that one of his fellow branch secretaries, at Wellingborough, was unfortunately killed in a car accident on the motorway. He found working at Biggleswade was good, as the majority of the team gelled together and all mucked in when needed; bus life there was like being in a close family. Mick also played darts for the depot, which gave him an opportunity to visit other depots for games, and to

Driver Stewart Crawley in the new depot messroom at Biggleswade. *Roger Warwick collection*

meet other busmen and women.

Mick and his colleagues used to cover turns in Bedford to help out in times of staff shortage. One driver he remembers conducting to was Rodney Davies from Northampton. At that time Rodney was not used to the routes in town and neither was Mick. They felt that they coped well, but it was a case of 'the blind leading the blind'. Mick remembers a 12-hour shift he once did in a manual-gearboxed minibus; he found it very hard on his shoulders and was lucky not to have one again, preferring vehicles with semi-automatic gearboxes.

Biggleswade crews also used to cover work at Hitchin and Huntingdon when required; Biggleswade and Huntingdon were sub-depots to Bedford, while Hitchin was a sub-depot of Luton. Other work involved duplicate coaches for scheduled services. Mick remembers working trips empty to Victoria Coach Station and duplicate services to the West Country. They also did work for the MOD, moving troops around the country. He remembers that one day he was part of a convoy of 35 double-deckers from Windsor Barracks to Heathrow Airport for an exercise called Operation 'Lionheart'. Twenty-one days later he went back with a coach and was delivering troops from Heathrow to Grantham and Lincoln; he remembers calling in at his home on one empty run for breakfast, before continuing. The whole job lasted from Friday lunchtime to Sunday teatime.

Bedford coach 260 was thinner than other coaches and was used on the Bedford Prison runs. It has since been sold on and is still working in Cambridgeshire, now painted red and cream. Other buses that Mick remembers were the Bristol LHs 404 and 408, the latter being a 'flyer'. 426 was a Bristol RESL and was easier to get round tight village roads than a standard RELL. The Bedford-chassised vehicles were from an MOD contract that had been cancelled after the chassis were built, and at times of bus shortages these were a good stopgap. Mick liked them because they had power-assisted steering.

When Stagecoach took over Mick worked with them until 1989, then returned to a career on the railways until retiring in November 2007. Two fellow drivers also retired then, Mike Hall and Stewart Crawley. Another, Brian Smith, moved from Biggleswade to Bedford.

Fred Campion

Mrs Campion, who has supplied these memories, is a local girl, but Fred was born in Berkshire. He came up to Biggleswade with his family from Ramsgate during the Second World War, starting work with Mantles, then at the local cinema. He was then called up to go to war, after which he was offered his job back at the cinema, but went to the Greene King brewery instead.

Fred was advised of a job on the buses by George

Pepper, who was a conductor at the time, but after two years he gave it up and became a bookbinder with Adams & Harrison. He could not settle there either, so went back on the buses, this time staying for 27 years until he retired in 1975 due to ill health at the age of 52.

When Fred became a driver he had a regular conductor called Les Hart. Another of the local drivers was Bill Gravestock, who had moved to United Counties from Bartles Coaches.

Fred enjoyed doing the annual tree-lopping job. The United Counties bus used to travel around the depots and volunteers would spend a week at a time cutting back trees on local bus routes. This no longer happens, as the owners have to cut the trees back themselves.

Later in his bus career he was appointed an Inspector, but did not like the early starts that this job entailed; he had to be at the depot early to open up and check in all the crews.

Biggleswade bus men and women used to be involved in day trips organised by themselves and the bus company. They would go free, but the children had to be paid for. However, the local children's home used to be invited to send its children on these trips. The Biggleswade families also used to be invited to the Bedford children's

parties, held in the Cornmarket, travelling there by bus.

Some of the local bus social events were held in the Old Labour Hall in Chapelfields. Others were held in the public house in Potton Road, where Ms Christine Booth used to entertain with a singing bird and singing herself. Another venue was the George's Hall, where Jim and Dennis Burley used to organise

Fred Campion, Fred Rook and Maurice Jewitt at one of the company award dinners. *Mrs Campion collection*

Conductress Mrs M. Housden receives an award from Mike Carr. Included in those looking on (from the left) are Bill Gravestock, Len Palastonja, George Dashwood, Derrick Merry, Sam Jones, Stan Bull, Peter Rayner, Les Bidewell and Lyn Worboys, with Fred Campion on the extreme right. *Mrs Campion collection*

dances, again raising money for local charities. Most years United Counties entered a bus as a float in the local carnival, also raising money for charity.

Fred was very active in the local bus social scene and was on the committee of the Social Club. He was also a sick visitor for the Welfare Club.

Lyn Worboys

I joined United Counties at Biggleswade Depot in Shortmead Street on 11 June 1966 at the age of 18. In those days you had to serve for three years as a conductor before becoming eligible to train as a driver. As the minimum age for a driver was 21, it did not cause me any concern.

After applying for a job to the Inspector in Charge, Mr Derek Merry (who lived locally in Holme

Cutting the cake is Tommy Hope at his 91st birthday party with colleagues at Biggleswade and Bedford depots. Also present are J. Spinks, J. Burton, N. W. Gravestock, Jim Burley, Mrs Christine Booth, G. Jones, Les Bidewell and R. Whitmore. *George W. Skevington, Dick Watson collection*

Fred on the left, with Mike Carr, Harold Johnson, Brian Horner and Maurice Jewitt leading the community singing at a Biggleswade social event. *Mrs Campion collection*

One of the Christmas parties. Fred Finding is at the back of the photograph. *Mrs Campion collection*

Court Avenue, Biggleswade) I was interviewed by the District Traffic Superintendent, Mr Maurice Jewitt, who was based at Bedford Depot. Two weeks later I started my conductor training at Bedford Depot, where I spent three days learning all about Setright ticket machines, waybills, parcels tickets and everything else that was required to conduct a bus. This training was based on the principle that the conductor was in charge of the bus and was responsible for its timekeeping when in service. My next three days were spent 'on the road', under the supervision of Biggleswade Depot's Conductor Instructor, Mr Fred Rook, and his driver Fred Finding.

After this training I was on my own; my first shift was on a Sunday, a late turn, and my first journey was the 4.30 'rounder'. This term was given to the duty that ran service 183 to Hitchin, then 182 from Hitchin to Bedford and return, followed by the 183 return to Biggleswade. A 'half rounder' was a duty that ran the 183 to Hitchin, then the 182 to Bedford, returning on service 176 to Biggleswade via Sandy; this took an hour less to do. These three services were operated in this form until Biggleswade Depot closed in 1991. The depot was then knocked down and flats built instead, which I recorded on camera for posterity. Biggleswade subsequently became an out-station of Bedford Depot. Initially it had 12 vehicles, later increased to a peak of 29. The new out-station was by the A1 flyover to the south of the town.

When I started at Biggleswade in 1966 the fleet consisted of 17 vehicles, three single-deckers and the rest double-deckers:

Bristol LS5G 441 (HBD 630), 442 (HBD 631) and 494 (LBD 258)
Bristol KS5G 834 (FRP 688), 835 (FRP 689), 836 (FRP 690), 837 (FRP 691) and 840 (FRP 695)
Bristol FS6B 672 (CNV 672B), 673 (CNV 673B) and 707 (GRP 707D)
Bristol FS6G 708 (HBD 708D) and 709 (HBD 709D)
Bristol LD5G 507 (NBD 906), 508 (NBD 907), 519 (NBD918) and 523 (NBD 922)

The depot was staffed by some 40 drivers and conductors under Derek Merry. George Theobalds was the Depot Engineer and Herbert Gray the Inspector (who had transferred from Bartles Coaches in 1953). The fitters were Jim Battson, Bernard Izzard and Jack Henderson, with cleaners Ernie Cook, Reg Scott and Freddie Gamble.

The drivers I remember include Fred Finding, Reg Finding, Geoff Giddings, Joe Tyson (my driver), Fred Campion, George Wildgoose, Peter Wilkinson, Brian Phillips, Roy Phillips, 'Taddy' Offin, Brian Ambrose, Maurice Endersby, Bernard Gudgin, 'Andy' Anderson, Bill Chenery (who died in 2006 aged 101), Rodney Albone, Fred Whitfield and Ron Chambers.

The conductors were Kit Wilkins, Velda Parker, Violet Jones, Barbara Cole, Ellen Clutton, Fred Rook, George Dashwood, Leslie Hart, Ron Robinson, Reg Pates, Ron Norris and George Duggan. Kit

Mrs Wildgoose at one of the Christmas parties. Driver George Wildgoose and his family emigrated to Australia, but when he died his wife came back home to Biggleswade.

More Biggleswade families enjoying the party. *Mrs Campion collection*

Wilkins's husband George ('Wilkie') had recently retired at this time. They lived at Arrington Bridge, which was the home of the Cambridge Blue bus service operated by Mr J. Goates, who ran a route from Cambridge to Bedford via Orwell, Arrington, Biggleswade and Sandy. Mr Goates sold out to Eastern National on 13 August 1934 and it became Eastern National route 29A, subsequently becoming United Counties route 175 on 1 May 1952. 'Wilkie' had been a driver for Cambridge Blue, where he had got to know my father, who travelled on his bus from Croydon (Cambs), my home village, to work at car dealers Marshalls of Cambridge. He subsequently worked for Eastern National and United Counties being transferred to Bedford Depot's outstation (one double-decker) at Cambridge, although he continued to live in Arrington.

In 1966 the routes operated by Biggleswade Depot were very different from today (2008). The only former routes that remain today are the 176 (Biggleswade-Sandy-Willington-Bedford), which was then hourly and is now the M3, running every 30 minutes, and the 179 (Biggleswade-Upper Caldecote-Ickwell-Northill-Bedford), then running infrequently but now running hourly as the M4.

One of the Biggleswade busmen as a children's entertainer. *Mrs Campion collection*

Driver Brian Phillips, on Bristol RELL 307 from Biggleswade Depot, drops off a lady in Cambridge Drummer Street Bus Station in 1974. *Lyn Worboys collection*

The other daily services used to be:

175: Biggleswade-Wrestlingworth-Arrington-Orwell-Harlton-Cambridge
177: Biggleswade-Bedford direct, Monday to Friday
180: Biggleswade-Broom-Stanford-Southill-Ireland-Haynes-Bedford
181: Biggleswade-Broom-Southill-Stanford-Clifton-Shefford, Saturday only
182: Hitchin-Arlesey-Henlow-Clifton-Shefford-Cotton End-Bedford
183: Biggleswade-Langford-Henlow-Arlesey-Letchworth-Baldock
184: Biggleswade-Edworth-Hinxworth-Astwick-Stotfold-Letchworth-Hitchin, Tuesday only
185: Biggleswade-Langford-Henlow-Arlesey-Letchworth-Baldock, Monday to Saturday only
185: Biggleswade-Southill-Shefford-Arlesey-Letchworth-Baldock, Monday to Saturday only
186: Baldock-Radwell-Stotfold-Arlesey-Henlow-Henlow Camp, Monday to Friday only
188: Biggleswade-Edworth-Hinxworth-Ashwell-Guilden Morden-Steeple Morden-Litlington-
     Abington Piggotts-Bassingbourn-Kneesworth-Royston-Reed-Buckland-Chipping-
     Buntingford, Wednesday and Saturday only
190: Biggleswade-Sutton-Potton-Everton-Gamlingay-Little and Great Gransden-Abbotsley-
     Eynesbury-St Neots
193: Biggleswade-Beeston-Sandy-Tempsford-Little Barford-Eynesbury-St Neots, Thursday and
     Saturday only – on the Saturday journey St Neots to Sandy was run by Huntingdon
     Depot
194: Waresley-Gamlingay-Potton-Everton-Sandy-Moggerhanger-Bedford, Wednesday, Saturday
     and Sunday only
195: Biggleswade-Sutton-Potton-Gamlingay-Hatley St George-East Hatley, Thursday and
     Saturday only
197: Biggleswade town service, Monday to Saturday only
214: St Neots-Duloe-Staploe, Thursday only

In addition, Biggleswade ran some short-workings on the following routes operated by Hitchin Depot:

88: Meppershall-Shillington-Pirton-Hitchin, Monday to Saturday only
91: Guilen Morden-Ashwell-Newnham-Letchworth-Hitchin, Monday to Friday only
94: Baldock-Letchworth-Hitchin, Monday to Friday only
97: Stotfold-Wilbury-Letchworth-Works Road, Monday to Friday only
98: Stotfold-Norton-Letchworth Station, Monday to Friday only

…and these Huntingdon depot services:

211: St Neots-Great Paxton-Offord Darcy-Offord Gurney (Swan), Thursday only
213: St Neots-Abbotsley-Great Gransden-Little Gransden-Caxton, Thursday only

On Sunday evenings up to two double-deckers, full of families going for a good night out, used to go to the pictures in St Neots on service 190. The drivers and the conductors also went into the cinema, which was free for them. One of the buses then did the last bus to Gamlingay that night before going back to the depot.

A notable event in the early 1970s was when Miss Georgina Hill, who lived in Stratton Way, Biggleswade, became United Counties' first woman bus driver (certainly in modern times, anyway), with Anglia Television visiting the depot to film her in action. Another event at about the same time was when *On the Buses* star Michael Robbins (Arthur Rudge, Stan's brother-in-law) paid a visit to the Travel Shop to borrow a Setright ticket machine so he could be photographed at a fete at nearby St Andrew's Church in Shortmead Street.

Biggleswade depot received one of the first batch of Bedford YRQ single-decker buses delivered to United Counties. It arrived on a Saturday morning in December 1973 and, after being checked by fitter Bernard Izzard, I was the first driver to operate it that day on the 15.45 service 190 journey to St Neots, then on the St Neots town service 209 before returning to Biggleswade.

During the late 1970s and early 1980s the depot became involved with express work. It had operated a Summer Saturday service to Great Yarmouth for many years. When I started, the express/private hire rota consisted of Fred Campion, George Wildgoose, Roy Phillips and Maurice Endersby. When Maurice left, in the early 1970s, I took over from him. One day Derek Merry, by now Depot Manager, called me into the office and asked, on behalf of Head Office, if we could supply a duplicate vehicle that Friday

Biggleswade staff: Standing, left to right, are Bill Barley, Frank Leonard, George Lawson, Eric Simmons, Gordon Jeeves, Fred Campion, Bob Young, Kit Wilkins, Alec Atkins, Frank Wilkins, Cyril Smith and Tommy Hope. Sitting, from the left, are Cyril Woods, Alf Askham, George Hallybone, a road safety officer, Gwen Derout and Bill Darlow. *Dick Watson collection*

Mr J. A. Birks traffic manager presents Mrs Wilkins (conductress) with her retirement gifts.

Retired driver C. Jeeves accepts his retirement presentation from Mr J. A. Birks, traffic manager.

Mr E. G. Dravers general manager congratulates driver A. F. Askham on his 21 years' Safe Driving award.

Conductor F. A. Rook receives his Safe Conducting Awards (24 years) from Mr E. G. Dravers general manager.

Biggleswade awards, from NBC News.

on the 16.30 Leicester to London Victoria service 555 and would I drive it? I stated that I had never been to London in my life, but would have a go. That Friday I set off for Leicester in RELH6G/ECW 284 (TBD 284G). I arrived at Southgates Coach Station and picked up almost a full load and, after picking up at Market Harborough, left Northampton Bus Station fully seated. Not having the speed of the Northampton Depot service Bristol RELH coach, I was left behind, and when I arrived at the capital I eventually found myself in Victoria Coach Station, the passengers directing me along Buckingham Palace Road to find it – they were very sympathetic!

Duplicates on services 550 and 555 became regular Friday and Saturday runs for us in both directions and at different times. We operated these services for several years, virtually all being driven by Ken Endersby and myself. Huntingdon and Bedford Depots also got involved in this work.

I soon became a regular visitor to London, sometimes several times a week, as our depot became heavily involved with private hire work. This was generated by the majority of schools in the Biggleswade, Sandy, Potton, Northill and Haynes areas. We also drove for many clubs and societies, including British Aerospace at Stevenage, Greene King Brewery in Biggleswade and W. H. Smith Travel in Bedford, and Harpenden hired us for all its theatre trips. We also drove that depot's British and continental holiday coaches. I was the first Biggleswade driver to go to the continent when I took a party from Haynes on a weekend to Belgium using Leyland Leopard/Duple Dominant IV 189(NNH 189Y).

We frequently borrowed coaches from Luton, Bedford, Hitchin (219) and Huntingdon (231). It was also not unknown to have seven or eight vehicles out on private hire on a Saturday. We even had Bristol VRs venturing as far as Folkestone, Lincoln, Great Yarmouth, Skegness and Clacton, as well as frequent visits to London.

I believe that, in the first half of the 1980s, Biggleswade and Kettering Depots were making the biggest profit on the private hire work. In later years this work became more cut-throat and the Board decided to pull out of it except for special jobs.

With deregulation in 1986, Biggleswade, under new manager Bob White, was successful in gaining extra work without losing any existing jobs.

The new jobs were:

91: Baldock-Newnham-Ashwell-Guilden Morden-Steeple Morden-Abbington Piggotts-Litlington-Bassingbourn-Kneesworth-Royston
91: Royston town service: Bus Station to Burns Road Estate
88: Hitchin-Gosmere-Preston-Kings Walden-St Paul Walden-Breachwood Green-Tea Green- Cockernhoe-Luton
189: Henlow-Arlesey-Stotfold – a peak-hour service linking with London trains at Arlesey station, with three journeys in the morning and three in the afternoon
303c: Hitchin-Wymondley-Stevenage
314: Hitchin-St Ippolits-Rush Green-Langley-Codicote-Welwyn-Welwyn Garden City

Services 88 and 91 had previously been operated by Luton & District Transport, which still had some short-workings on the 91 between Hitchin and Steeple Morden, while London Country North East had an early morning and early evening journey between the same points. Service 189 was a new service under the control of Bedfordshire County Council, being experimental for train connections. Services 303c and 314 were previously run by London Country North East, 314 being an all-day service while the 303c was a works service running

Georgina Hill, the first woman bus driver at Biggleswade, is seen here with Teddy Dravers. *NBC News*

in Stevenage via the Gunnels Wood Road industrial area and only at peak times. Two Leyland Nationals were required for service 88 and one Leyland National for 189 (morning), then service 91 all day, finishing with the 189 afternoon journeys. One Bristol VR operated the early morning 303c journey, then 314 all day and the return 303c journey before finishing with the 17.40 Hitchin to Welwyn on the 314. These four vehicles were out-stationed at Holwell near Hitchin, coming under Biggleswade.

Coming up to date, in 2008 services 88, 91 and 314 were operated by Centrebus after a brief spell with Arriva Shires & Essex, while routes 189 and 303c no longer existed.

In September 1995 Stagecoach United Counties won 25 Cambridgeshire school contracts, formerly operated by Whippet coaches; most of these were in the Huntingdon and St Neots areas. As a result, Huntingdon Depot received 11 more vehicles. At the same time Biggleswade received five vehicles, four to cover the Cambridgeshire work and one to cover Huntingdon work transferred to Biggleswade. This contract was from Arrington via Wimpole, Orwell, New Wimpole and Whaddon to Bassingbourn Village College, and Whaddon and Arrington Bridge to Orwell Petersfield School. The afternoon return also had a new contract from Comberton Village College to Great and Little Eversden in front of it, before running dead to Orwell.

Biggleswade also operated other contracts to and from Comberton Village College and Bourn Junior School. Another ran from St Neots Longsands School to Little Paxton and from Gamlingay via Waresley, Great and Little Gransden, Abbotsley, Graveley and Yelling into Huntingdon Technical College.

In 2006 Biggleswade Depot lost a great deal of work. The town services were subsequently operated by Herberts Travel of Shefford, ironically with former Stagecoach Mercedes 709Ds, and the 200 service to Flitwick by Grant Palmer of Dunstable, who also ran the 197 Tuesday 'Shopper' service to Milton Keynes. Centrebus also then ran the hourly 82 service from Hitchin to Biggleswade. Centrebus took over Arriva services 88, 91 and 314 and all town services, except the 81 to Westmill, and as a result Arriva closed the former United Counties Hitchin Depot, which is awaiting demolition. Arriva also lost a number of services in Stevenage to Centrebus, with the 315 service from Codicote to Welwyn Garden City and the 390 service from Stevenage to Ware.

I can remember the day we lost most of the fleet to a fire. It was suspected as arson, but could not be proved. Replacement vehicles came from all over the country to keep us going. We ran all the services, but were unable to use some of the ticket machines.

The Biggleswade outstation went back down to 14 vehicles, three fewer than when I started in 1966 and with a lot less overheads. These vehicles included six ADL Dart SLFs for the 'MARS' M1-M4 services There were also two step-entrance Darts, one for schools service 201 (Henlow Camp-Meppershall-Shillington-Gravenhurst-Shefford-Haynes-Bedford). There were five S-registered Volvo Olympians, 16223/4/5/7/9 (S753 DRP, etc), and two Volvo B10M coaches, in yellow 'Schooliner' livery, 52368/9 (P168/9 KBD).

The buildings at Biggleswade are let out to Hamilton Cars, which has been there since 1996, while Bedfordshire County Council Social Services also park six vehicles at the depot. The Biggleswade compound also occasionally holds Stagecoach vehicles held in reserve or awaiting disposal; the premises are owned by Stagecoach.

The staff at Biggleswade consists of me, Terry Williams and John Elt, all leading drivers, and permanent school bus drivers John Robertson, Richard Scholes, Cliff Dixon, Richard Peters, Alan Payne and Mary Houghton. The other drivers are Derek Hallibone, Ian Warland, Paul Sabey, Dennis Hann, Iain Godfrey, Malcolm Bradburn, Brian Fountain, Martin Smith, Darren Moor, Terry Auburn and Trevor Broggi. The majority of these drivers have been with the company for many years and live nearby.

Lyn Worboys and fitter Colin Tyler with their preservation project. *NBC News*

4
Bletchley

Bletchley was originally the sub-depot to Stony Stratford but later became the more important of the two. It was eventually replaced by the new Milton Keynes Depot at Winterhill.

Alan Parfitt

Alan remembers that Bletchley services used single-deckers, due to the low railway bridges. However, on Saturday double-deckers were used, which terminated short on the other side of the station. He recalls that one of the inspecting staff was Reg Foreman; their job was to check in the staff, do the day-to-day rostering and offer overtime when needed. When the enquiry office was closed they used to take the enquiry telephone calls; breakdown emergencies were also dealt with, informing the mechanical foreman and organising the recovery. Another of the Inspectors was Norman Midgeley, and George Newman's wife worked as the telephonist and receptionist in the office. She also dealt with the lost property, and Alan remembers covering for her when at lunch.

Graham Cumming

Graham was working for Seamarks when he decided to apply for a driving job with United Counties at Bletchley's Tavistock Road Depot in 1977. He was one of the first one-person-operation drivers at Bletchley. The main bus used was the Bristol RELL, of which Bletchley had four at that time of a total of about 14 buses. The rest were Bristol FLF and VR double-deckers, which were used on the 50 and 51 routes round Bletchley, travelling up and down Whaddon Way. About 30 crews worked out of Tavistock Street.

This was a time when the centre of Milton Keynes had not been built and new estates were still being built around Bletchley. Serving the two new estates of Netherfield and Bean Hill, Bletchley Depot ran buses that had cardboard cut-out passengers on the top deck to give the impression that they carried many more passengers than they did.

Graham remembers that the main country route was the Bletchley to Oxford rail replacement service,

Tavistock Street Depot, Bletchley. *Roger Warwick collection*

Albert Street Depot, the old bakery. *Roger Warwick collection*

which was manned by Bletchley crews. The buses originated in Cambridge and ran via Bedford.

In 1978 United Counties outgrew Tavistock Road Depot and moved to the old bakery building. The facilities there were very sparse, with one pit and two fitters, and the offices were in Portakabins. Graham does not remember there being any heating at the depot either. At this time the Dial-a-Bus minibuses were introduced, which greatly enhanced the fleet;

they were later moved to a special unit near Wavendon Towers and the Open University, where they had their own control centre.

The nearest depot to Bletchley was Stony Stratford. However, the crews did not talk to each other, and later on, when they all moved to Winterhill, they would gravitate to their own parts of the canteen, still being reluctant to mix with each other. While Stony Stratford remained separate, it mainly

Bletchley Bus Station, with the Portakabin offices ('The Hut'). *Roger Warwick collection*

operated local service and works runs, interspersed with the odd country route to Northampton and occasionally Bletchley.

By 1978 there were 30 vehicles at Bletchley Depot, including eight coaches. New Bristol VR buses were 799 to 801, which were superior to previous vehicles, and 800, which was a 'dud' bus and was shunted off to Stony Stratford as quickly as possible.

Graham remembers that his Bletchley Inspector was Brian Bailey and that the man in charge was Albert Lambert. Richard Christian was the Area Manager, who later moved to Ribble and sadly died at the age of 34. Graeme Carr was Depot Superintendent; he later took up posts at Head Office at Northampton and still works for Stagecoach East, and his job was taken on by Nick Smith, who had been doing the graphs and charts for bus rotas.

Graham rapidly rose to Inspector in 1979 at Stony Stratford, moving back to Bletchley in 1982. At that time all buses were one-person-operated, including the depot's first woman driver, Mrs Ann Tuffen. Road staff now totalled 50, which was a drop due to the loss of all conductors and conductresses.

The staff at Bletchley were very much used to their own way of doing work and did not like change.

Ann Tuffen was the first conductress to learn to drive a bus at Bletchley, but she was not allowed on the road until managers and union officials had resolved various issues. *Northampton Chronicle & Echo*

Graeme Carr

December 1978 was the end of Graeme's training and he was given a job at Milton Keynes. This was a very interesting time there as the new city was under construction and it was envisaged that a large fleet of buses would be required. Stony Stratford and Bletchley were the local depots, and Graeme's office was at Bletchley Bakery (Albert Street) Depot. Servicing was carried out at the old depot, which was much smaller. Graeme was also responsible for Stony Stratford, which involved bringing the two sets of staff together, who historically did not get on. Even when a new depot was built and the others closed, the staff still used different parts of the canteen. Bletchley had 29 vehicles and Stony Stratford 17, and each depot had an Inspector in Charge.

Bletchley ran mainly local services and the joint run to Stony Stratford and Wolverton. Stony Stratford was again mainly works services, locals and Northampton runs.

A new bus station and depot were opened at Winterhill in 1983, by the railway station but away from the main shopping centre. Unfortunately, the depot was underused for the whole of its career.

New services had started using FLF vehicles in the 400/410/420 and 440 series. Dial-a-Bus buses formed a separate unit based at Wavendon Towers, which later transferred to the Bakery. Bristol RELL vehicles were used on local services, and the Bristol FLFs were replaced by Bristol VRs.

In the early 1980s Graeme became involved in the preservation scene with the ownership of former London Transport SMS 683. When an open day was held at Winterhill, Graeme's bus had the shortest journey, all of 50 feet from inside the depot to the yard!

Jack and Betty Bootle

Jack was born in Wigan and could not find work, so he moved to London under a Government scheme, his allowance enabling him to have five Woodbines and a library book a week after paying his bills. He volunteered for active service during the Second World War and became an artilleryman for a year;

however, as he was a trained engineer he was called back for war work, finding employment as a milling machine operator at Electroflow in Park Royal, a factory making meters and periscopes. This is where the Bootles met.

After the war Jack was made redundant and applied to London Transport to work at its Chiswick Works. However, he was taken on as a conductor instead, working out of Willesden Garage. Here there was a rule that if any member of the road staff appeared without headgear, he or she was sent home without pay. Jack remembered this all his driving and inspecting life and very rarely was seen without a hat.

In 1954 the Bootles were given the chance of a new house in Bletchley and a job at United Counties. They corresponded with Mr Partridge, the Depot Superintendent at Stony Stratford, and with the company at Northampton.

When they arrived in Bletchley, their daughter Jean was only six weeks old and they found a change of home and family status a handful. Their second daughter, Brenda, arrived four years later, by which time they had become established in the area.

Jack started as a driver, with a pay rate of 2s 4¼d per hour. He was a tough Lancastrian and for a short time became the union representative at Bletchley. He fought with and on behalf of his colleagues to obtain company pensions for all bus people, which did not make him too popular with managers, but he was a family man first and a socialist second, so this was not a problem.

Jack did not like being interrupted when he was doing his paperwork. One day a Milton Keynes road-planning official was looking over his shoulder and Jack told him to 'bugger off'!

Jack worked out of Tavistock Street and the Bakery Depots before Winterhill was built; the Bakery Depot was next to the bus station, which made life a bit easier when problems arose.

Many of the drivers and conductors lived on the same estate as the Bootles. A private arrangement was used by which the driver of the last bus would leave it outside the morning driver's house, then walk home. When one of the Inspectors found out, this short-cut was stopped immediately.

Some of Jack's colleagues were drivers Peter New, Mick Coughlan, Bill Phillips, Dan Young, Clarry White and Teddy Fisk, and the conductors and conductresses included Mrs Carter, Lil Morgan and Cyril Gornel. Mrs Carter was a clippie when the Bootles arrived and carried on for many years before leaving.

Mrs Bootle remembers several of the Inspectors, including mobile inspector Jeff Manning from Northampton, Brian Bailey, also from Northampton, who relieved when one of the others was on holiday, and Heather Chilton, who was the first female United Counties Inspector. Later Jack himself was promoted

Letters to Jack when he moved to United Counties at Bletchley. *Bootle family collection*

to Inspector, and his first month's work was at Stony Stratford, before he returned to Bletchley.

Two of his work memories relate to unusual incidents. Milton Keynes has an entertainment centre called the National Bowl, and when the pop group, the Police, appeared United Counties provided vehicles to transport the fans. The rain did not stop all day and Jack came home with his trousers very muddy. He suggested to the Superintendent that he should have a new uniform, and was disgusted when he was given a

Jack Bootle and Harry Shipton (or Shipley), having a rest between duties. *Bootle family collection*

Inspector Jack Bootle. *Bootle family collection*

The first woman Inspector at Bletchley was Heather Chilton. *NBC News*

Sketchley cleaning voucher instead! The buses used got a steam clean as well, being covered inside and out with mud.

The other memory was a frightening experience. Jack was on duty at Bletchley bus station hut one night when a gale blew up. The adjacent office block was clad in plastic sheeting, which came off and flew around the whole area. They were acting like razor blades, and Jack brought the two or three waiting passengers in with him to stop them being hit by the panels. Eventually all were rescued.

Long-service awards: the back row includes Dick Watson, Mick Draper, George Rowney and Bob Rumbold, and the front row includes John Tate, Fred Dark, Irwin Dalton, George Carruthers and Jack Bootle (extreme right). *Bootle family collection*

Jack was awarded a medal for 25 years' service and attended a dinner in Northampton to receive it. When he retired in 1982 he received a clock from Irwin Dalton. When Jack died his winter uniform was sent to Bosnia to help keep someone else warm – thus a United Counties Inspector might have been wandering around Eastern Europe without knowing it!

The family have retained all Jack's cap badges, including the pre-1957 straight one with a half circle in the centre, the post-1957 round ones, his Inspector's badge and later National Bus Company badges, in remembrance of his work with United Counties.

Mrs Bootle remembers drivers Pat Broderick, Linda Chown, Fred Crockett, the union man, and conductors Harry Davies and Sid Joyce. She also remembers that the Inspector in Charge was Albert Lambert.

Irwin Dalton presents Jack with a clock on his retirement. *Bootle family collection*

5
Corby

Corby was a sub-depot of Kettering and became more important as the village became a town with the opening of the steelworks.

Corby Depot in National Bus Company days, with visiting Barton coaches. *Roger Warwick collection*

Brian Hadden

Brian has worked for United Counties and Stagecoach for 35 years, most of them at Corby as garage cleaner/shunter, fitter's mate (running repairs), crew driving in overtime hours and OMO driver, Inspector, Assistant Manager to Bill Smith, then Manager at Kettering. He is now Operations Manager North Northants, covering Kettering and Corby with all outstations. Brian's box number at Corby was 22, and he still has that on his company rule book.

At Corby the pit had a grille over the top. When it rained outside the pit filled up and would overflow into the rest of the depot, requiring pumping out. The MOT examiner in the Corby days was Mr Stone, who would come over and do spot checks

Brian has taken many photographs over the years at both Kettering and Corby, some of which appear in this book. Here he is at the launch of Corby STAR buses 28 May 2003.

The bus station at Corby steelworks. *Roger Warwick collection*

occasionally, involving Brian in physical and written work. George Mair was the Chargehand Fitter at this time. The Corby staff included a fitter and mate with two male and two female cleaners.

Corby's work seemed to revolve around the steelworks. This had its own bus station, and buses left soon after 6.00am, 2.00pm and 10.00pm daily. The only Sunday services were run from this bus station. The Tube Mills had buses at 7.00am, 3.00pm and 11.00pm. Buses went to all local areas, with up to 14 of the Corby allocation used.

At Corby's bus station the crews had a canteen and toilets, which was better than at the depot.

Today Brian still enjoys the company of his colleagues and works with the local authority to provide the best bus service his budget will allow. His secretary is Vivian Thompson, who has worked on and off for the company for many years. In 1998 she returned to do a variety of work including switchboard operator, typist and cash office clerk.

Mick Godsell

Mick has worked at Corby for many years and has contributed the accompanying photograph, from the *Corby Evening Telegraph*, which depicts the only country public service, running from Corby to Stamford, on 8 December 1976.

Corby staff were very good at winning competitions, including the National Driver of the Year competition. The second photograph shows the winning team in the Northamptonshire Better Driving Competition, which included a 60-mile driving course, tests in Kettering Cattle Market and answering questions from the Highway Code. Charles Simpson and Gordon

Corby's first bus station.
Roger Warwick collection

Mr and Mrs Len Ford and Bill Smith Snr are seen on the occasion of Len's retirement, backed by Corby staff including Duncan McBlain, Mary Swanson, John Burns, Sid Quayle, Lenny Fennel, Stan Grantham, Mick Godsell, Ann Smith and Obrad Djukic. *Corby Evening Telegraph, Mick Godsell collection*

Osborne were the overall winners, Tim Roberts won a trophy, and they all won the Team Trophy.

Neil Tayton

Neil has worked at Corby for 2½ years driving the Kettering and Corby rail-link bus, which is at the time of writing sponsored by East Midlands Trains, a Stagecoach company. He found the Magic Mini buses a problem in Corby, as the passengers used to request stops at what appeared to be every 10 feet! However, when all-day tickets were introduced this saved much time at stops.

Other memories

Ralph Money has worked for Stagecoach since 1988, as a driver at both Northampton and Corby. Before that he worked at Seven Kings and Upton Park for London Transport; he was a conductor for 14 years on AEC Routemasters on the 15 route from East Ham to Ladbrooke Grove.

   William Lawson also worked as a driver and instructor at Corby until being made redundant a couple of years ago. He still has good contacts with John Appleton, Mick Hearn, Steve Payne, David Haynes, Tom Poulter, Tim Roberts, John Letch Snr, John Storey (electrician) and Frank Howell.

Robin Hopkins, Tim Roberts, Charles Simpson, Gordon Osborne, Ruby Knox and Conn McEleney with medals after a car rally in August 1974. *Corby Evening Telegraph*

The introduction of the Magic Minis: driver Kaisar Singh, Mayor Ron Hopkiss and Tony Cox. *Kettering Evening Telegraph*

6
Daventry

Daventry was a sub-depot of Northampton.

Mick Crisp

Mick has been a driver at Daventry and Northampton for many years. When he started with United Counties he had to get a union card first, then be put on a waiting list. He remembers many colleagues at Daventry, including drivers Ron Waldock, Arthur Hart, George Conroy, John Thompson, Trevor Turner and Ernie Snoad, and conductors Phyllis Hannant (who went to Cromer), Mary Machin and Peter Waldock (who became a driver).

Buses at Daventry included one single-decker (known as a 'tram') and three double-deckers. The first bus out in the morning was 6.00am to Long Buckby and Watford on the 306, and the first town service was out at 6.35am. The Daventry-Northampton buses were route 311. Mick remembers working with Cyril Nix, who lived at Long Buckby.

One duty was Daventry to Northampton, back to Long Buckby, Ravensthorpe, East Haddon, Harlestone and Northampton again. Another was a single-decker to Upper Weedon, where the bus turned at a pub (the Duke William). The landladies at the pub opened up at 7.00am and provided hot coffee and toast for the crew, while in the summer there was orange juice and cakes, and the busmen bought them Christmas presents as a thanks. At lunch times crews used to go to Adams's restaurant for a good meal before working home. Mick remembers going for lunch with John Thompson. Northampton to Daventry was 2s 6d return, and weekly tickets were 10 or 11 shillings.

After the 12.10pm return to Daventry there was the option of overtime on a school run, which paid a minimum of 3½ hours at a time-and-a-half pay rate. Also included with this run was dead mileage back to Northampton and a passenger return to Daventry.

Daventry Depot in National Bus Company days.
Steve Loveridge collection

Mick remembers that the Depot Superintendent at Derngate was Norman Maycock; other Derngate Inspectors were Peter Lewis, Len Chapman, Stan Palmer, Frank Harrison, Derek Mould and Brian Bailey. United Counties buses were well maintained, but freezing; more modern buses are warmer! One year Frank Harrison was Father Christmas, and went out on a bus to Chapel Brampton, but was left behind. He arrived back to Derngate on the back of a coal lorry.

Daventry Bus Station. *Steve Loveridge collection*

7
Desborough

Desborough is an out-station of Kettering.

David March

David has worked all over the north Northamptonshire area, but his memories start at Desborough where the depot was used as a fertiliser store for many years, and during the war was used to make warplanes.

The Desborough allocation was four saloon single-deckers and four double-deckers. Wages would arrive in a sandwich tin chained to the 2.30pm service 261 bus. Money was sent to Kettering where it was banked. One day the bank bus went to the wrong bank and it took ages to sort out the mess! Desborough's cleaner was Sandy Rolf.

David is the Pensions Representative at Kettering, with 122 staff on his books.

Derrick Fox

Derrick is currently a driver at Kettering, and remembers that one Desborough service went round the town before going on. One day the conductor, Reg Hunt, who was supposed to go into the depot and report before continuing, was left behind when the driver moved on after a bell sounded, not having realised that a passenger had rung it. At Braybrooke Derrick enquired where his conductor was and was told he had left him behind. Reg had walked back to Kettering Depot in the meantime.

Top: **Desborough Depot is on the left, with buses waiting while crews are inside.** *Alan Parfitt collection*

Left: **Desborough Depot, with the stores building on the left.** *Roger Warwick collection*

8
Hitchin

Hitchin was a sub-depot of Luton.

Stan and Robin Knight

Robin never officially worked for United Counties, but spent much time at Hitchin Depot with his father Stan. Stan had fought in Arnhem, and when he came home he worked on the buses. He started in 1954 with Birch Brothers, working out of Henlow on

the 203 route, then moved to United Counties. Even though he had passed a PSV test with Birch Brothers, he had to take another one at Castle Street, Luton, which entailed a trip round the block. A while later he left to drive sand lorries, but in 1965 he arrived back at United Counties, working out of Hitchin Depot.

One of Stan's main driving jobs was as outstation driver at Holwell. He and Bristol LS MAX 109 spent many hours working on the local runs

Hitchin Depot. *Roger Warwick collection*

Stanley Knight in the depot at Hitchin. *Robin Knight collection*

in the area. Being based at the local village hall, the bus was used unofficially for youth club trips to local villages. When the outstation closed, Stan returned to Hitchin. When the business was sold to Luton & District, he became a shareholder, which worked out well for him.

Hitchin conductors and conductresses finished work with the introduction of one-person-operation in 1980. Stan retired in 1991, and when he died a few years later his ashes were

Robin Knight preparing a Leyland National for its day's use. *Robin Knight collection*

transported back to Arnhem for burial.

Because of childcare problems Robin spent much time working with his father. His first recollections are of lying on the bench seats, at 18 months of age, with his sister while father drove around the county. The passengers provided the childcare and looked after the children well.

When Robin grew up he used to go into work with his father to prepare the bus together, and others if time allowed. Some drivers would be upset if their bus had been prepared, so Robin knew which ones to do and which ones to leave.

Robin remembers one occurrence when he and his father were on Leyland National 542 with a conductress called Terri. Inspector Higgins got on the bus and was very upset that Robin was travelling with his father. Robin had a pass, but the Inspector was upset as this was not Robin's but his father's.

The Leyland Nationals were too big for the country roads round Hitchin, and were always being bashed around by local trees and walls. On one occasion a car met Stan's bus, which was taking up three-quarters of the

road, and shot past, hit a drainage ditch, flew in the air and hit a car behind the bus. The passengers had the unusual sight of a car at bus level. The young driver was more worried about his father's reaction to his accident than being concerned about himself. Fortunately only the two cars were damaged and no people were injured.

Robin remembers some of the vehicles at Hitchin, particularly Bristol FS 716, Bristol RELLs 318, 321 and 322, and Bristol RELHs 207, 208, 209, 253 and 282. The RELHs were used on the 204 route to Bedford from Hitchin on Saturdays only. Route 203

Hitchin's 209 receives a wash from an unknown cleaner with new equipment. *Roger Warwick collection*

ran to Welwyn from Rushden, and the main driver on this route was Bill Almquest from Rushden. No excursions were run from Hitchin, due to an agreement with Tricentrol Coaches. Also remembered are Leyland Nationals 450, 451, 452, 504, 510, 511, 512, 513, 524, 532, 537, 548, 566, 581, 587, 588 and 589 and Bristol VRs 802 and 803, followed by 804 and 805, then 815. The VRs were low-height to go under Hitchin railway bridge. No 548 was the local bus for the disabled.

Hitchin Depot remained in use until January 2007, when its work was taken over by Arriva at Stevenage. Robin has his own bit of United Counties memorabilia, as he has preserved Leyland National 587, one of his father's favourites.

Alan Parfitt remembers that Hitchin had two Bristol LD5Gs, 519 and 520, which worked on Luton to Hitchin and Stotfold services. Drivers at Hitchin also ran services to Baldock via Letchworth. Timings were very tight: Luton to Hitchin in 30 minutes was difficult, 10 minutes from Hitchin to Letchworth was very difficult, and 10 minutes from Letchworth to Baldock was 'bloody impossible'!

Hitchin crews at Baldock. *Colin Routh and Alan Parfitt collections*

Hitchin Inspector Harold Barnsley receives his retirement present from Irwin Dalton and Colin Clubb. *Colin Clubb collection*

9
Huntingdon

Huntingdon Depot, with a bus leaving for duty. *Roger Warwick collection*

The Inspectors', then Controllers', office at Huntingdon, which was unusual for its all-round visibility. *Roger Warwick collection*

Huntingdon was a sub-depot of Bedford

Gerald Mead

When Gerald was young he remembers that the London General Bus Company ran services in

single-decker buses were 100, 101 and 102.

Huntingdon used to run the longest fare-stage service in that part of the country, from St Ives to Aylesbury (141). Huntingdon crews worked to Bedford and were then used on town service 101, brickworks workers' buses and Westbourne schools services, before returning to Huntingdon on another

Huntingdon Bus Station. *Roger Warwick collection*

Huntingdon with Leyland open-topped double-deckers.

He was working for British Railways as an engine driver at Huntingdon when the Beeching Report came out in about 1960. Huntingdon locomotive depot closed as a result and Gerald was made redundant. He then became a conductor with United Counties at Huntingdon.

At this time Huntingdon had 17 rotas for the buses; 14 were crew runs and three were one-person-operated. The 17 drivers, 14 conductors and other employees made a total of 40 staff at this time. The one-person-operated

141. The 141 ran every 2 hours and two Huntingdon and two Aylesbury buses were used. The last bus to Huntingdon left Bedford at 9.35pm and for Aylesbury at 8.35pm.

The original bus station, at Mill Common, consisted of a tin building and a series of bays with a telephone connection to the depot. A new bus station,

Bristol RELH 280 with Driver Bill McMordie and Gerald Mead inside Huntingdon Depot. *Gerald Mead collection*

the present Tilling-style building, was built while Gerald was the Superintendent.

While on the railways Gerald had been an official for the National Union of Railwaymen, and when he worked on the buses he transferred to the Transport & General Workers Union. He was active in the union and became a local then company delegate. This later post involved regular meetings at Northampton with other colleagues and the senior company managers. In these days he was working with Dennis Mulligan, Fred Moore and Des Banyard. He also remembers that Dick Cleavey was an influential person at Bedford.

Gerald was an acting road inspector in the early 1970s, on Mondays, Thursdays and Saturdays, being a full Inspector when his son Terry joined the company in 1973. At this time the television programme *On the Buses* was showing, and Gerald was rapidly nicknamed 'Blakey' after the character of the Inspector in the show. From this time Gerald remembers the husband and wife team of Bill and Maureen McMordie, who both worked for the company for more than 25 years.

In the early years Huntingdon was controlled by Maurice Jewitt from Bedford, who dealt with the hiring, firing and discipline. In later years this role was transferred to Luton, under Bob Rumbold,

Gerald Mead, Bob Rumbold and Bill and Maureen McMordie on Bill's retirement, with Dennis Mulligan, John Broughton and Brian McCall. *Gerald Mead collection*

Three of Huntingdon Depot's stalwarts, with between them 99 years of service: Joyce Wheeler, 'Curly' Musk and Stanley Tiller. *NBC News*

and later still to Gerald himself when Huntingdon became self-running. Gerald became the Depot Superintendent, taking over from Mr Spicer, who had worked at Huntingdon Depot for 47 years, and retired from that position in 1984. His post was taken on by Joe Hehir, and later by his son Terry Mead.

With its close proximity to the A1, Huntingdon vehicles were used to duplicate National Express services. The main service was the Victoria Coach Station to Newcastle service. One duplication entailed Bristol RELH dual-purpose coach 280 going to Edinburgh; 280 was the pet coach at Huntingdon, and replaced a broken-down Scottish vehicle, rescued by fitter Leach. Other Bristol coaches at Huntingdon were RELHs 255, 256 and 258, and MW coach 261. Later coaches were Leyland Leopards 205, 206 and 207.

The depot also had a comprehensive excursion programme. In 1975, for example, excursions varied in price from 50p for an evening mystery tour up to £2.40 for a trip to the Blackpool Illuminations. Blackpool trips usually loaded to three coaches, including office staff from Northampton. On summer Sundays a fare-stage service was run to Hunstanton for day-trippers. In 1983 this trip cost £3.00 and the loading sometimes meant that three

Driver 'Curly' Musk and Gerald Mead at Southend Coach Park with MW 203. *Gerald Mead collection*

'Curly' Musk and friend. *Dick Watson collection*

double-deckers and a coach went to the seaside. Sometimes a driver was seconded to drive there and back while taking his family out for the day.

Staff that Gerald remembers were drivers 'Curly' Musk and Mr West, driver trainer Stan Phillips, conductors Stan Tiller and Alfred Lane, engineers Paul Smith and Peter Griffiths, and Mechanical Foreman Jack Darlow.

Contract work was not regular in Gerald's day, but one job was eight double-deckers on a bus replacement service, a short MOD contract to Alconbury Air Base and works buses to Huntingdon

Richard Askew (Bedford), Gerald Mead, Conductress Miss Joyce Wheeler and Doug Elphee. *Gerald Mead collection*

Research Centre.

Most Huntingdon to Cambridge buses went via St Ives, while the Oxmoor Estate had 223/224 services, one clockwise and the other anti-clockwise.

Gerald felt that 95% of his staff were reliable and only 5% had to be watched. Huntingdon has always been short of staff, and as a result office staff worked on Saturdays, including Ray Ramsey, Steve Loveridge and Rod Davies. Dennis Mulligan used to relieve as a road inspector, checking loading on the excursions. Again due to staff shortages conductors used to work 12-hour days, and the equivalent pay on British Rail would be an 8-hour day. Spreadover duties were hated at Huntingdon.

At one time, in National Bus Company days, Eastern Counties outstationed buses at Huntingdon when it closed its St Ives Depot.

Bus-cleaning at Huntingdon improved; it started with a hosepipe and brush, followed by a portable rotating brush and later a standard two-brush bus, wash and pan.

Wages were drawn at Huntingdon and administered at Bedford, later Northampton.

Terry Mead

When Terry left school he worked as a draughtsman at Atcost agricultural systems in St Ives, followed by a job doing work study in a company in Huntingdon, before moving in with his father Gerald Mead at United Counties in Huntingdon, with a bang, on 5 November 1973.

Terry was a temporary conductor for two months, then took his driving test in February 1974. He remembers that the prestige service 141 only ran to Bedford in those days, while Bristol VR buses were used on the London Overspill estate at Oxmoor.

Terry spent four years (1989-93) as a Driving Instructor with John Appleton, then eight weeks in Perth with his own training bus SBD 545, training 40 staff. During this time he also worked in the Control Office (1992-93). The Chief Driving Instructor was Mr Cassidy, and Terry undertook one week's intensive training.

When Terry's father Gerald retired in 1985, Joe Hehir became Depot Manager. In 1993 the Depot Traffic Manager's job was given to Terry, and from that time he has run the depot, first for Stagecoach United Counties (1987-97), then MK Metro (Premier Buses) (1997-98), as Operations Manager for Blazefield buses (1998-2003) and from 2003 as part of the Cavalier contracts group. Terry is now the Manager for Huntingdon and Long Sutton Depots. In 2008 the company was back in the Stagecoach fold trading as Stagecoach in the Fens Ltd.

His latest project is working with the developers in producing the Cambridge guided busway, using the former St Ives railway corridor. This will help the local public and avoid the bottlenecks of the local main roads.

Before the end of the decade Terry will be transferring the depot to a larger site to incorporate facilities for the 63 drivers and extra engineering staff. The fleet has gone from 14 buses in his father's day to about 40 today; 11 vehicles are kept at outstations. Most of these work on the contract with one of the Cambridge colleges, and some are at Ely, Bishops Stortford, Mildenhall, Somersham and St Neots.

Ron Hannibal

Ron Hannibal joined the buses with London Transport when he left school, finishing up at Tottenham Garage as a driver. Ron drove most types of London buses, including FRM and RTL types.

In December 1968 the Hannibal family moved to Huntingdon, as they could not get a house in London and United Counties was recruiting. The family was also looking for a better standard of living than they could hope to have in London. Ron was interviewed by Maurice Jewitt, Manager at Bedford, who held interviews in the Elephant & Castle area for the Bedford, Biggleswade and Huntingdon areas. At that time Huntingdon Depot had mainly manual gearbox vehicles, which took much effort in comparison to the London Transport buses. Ron was to suffer the effects of using these boxes when he retired. When he started, the Manager at Huntingdon was Barry Hinde, who later moved on to other work later on. Mrs McMordie was in the office.

Ron made friends with two other drivers, Terry Mead and Melvyn Karley, and the three of them graduated to drive coaches on private hires, excursions and coach holidays; Ron especially remembers trips to Oban and Scarborough. On many long-distance trips two out of the three used to double up on the driving. Ron also remembers working in the Bedford area to help out in times of crew shortage, and trips to Northampton on the 128 service to Cambridge.

Ron became involved with the social side of work at Huntingdon and used to run the staff shop. He would buy all the tea, coffee, sweets, crisps and sugar at the local cash and carry and charge the staff initially 10 shillings a week for the service. This levy later rose to £1 a week each. Any profit at the end of the year was distributed to the staff who used the shop. However, he had to give up the shop when colleagues began not to pay anything for the goods. Ron had an honesty box for paying for sweets and crisps – some gave and others did not. Huntingdon also had darts and cricket teams, and Ron got involved with both.

Huntingdon drivers also used to compete in the United Counties Driver of the Year competitions, and Ron had a go at the Luton heat one year.

When United Counties had a Leyland National

Back row: Bob Carr, Derek Leach, Ron Perry, Barry Smith, Melvyn Karley, Keith Crawford, Dave Watson, Dave Phrimpton, Victor Heath, Tony Wheeler, Gordon Burnside, Melvin Leach, Terry Bradbury and Ron Hannibal. The front row includes Tracey Darline, Joe Hehir and Pearl Hehir. *Terry Mead collection*

Ron Hannibal with his manager/friend Terry Mead in May 1994 on the occasion of his retirement. *Gerald and Terry Mead collection*

converted for disabled people, Ron remembers taking a party from Spalding to the South Coast. Ron always enjoyed his work and misses the driving and meeting people. Later he drove for Stagecoach Coachlinks, on services from Peterborough to Heathrow Airport.

Ron retired in May 1994 and was presented with a leaving gift by his old friend Terry Mead, who was then the Manager of the depot. Many of his old colleagues have now died, and Ron is sorry that there are not enough of them left to have a reunion and talk about old times. He remembers taking the retired staff to Northampton for the annual reunions when they were held.

Victor Heath

Vic was born in Stoke on Trent in 1942, one of 13 children. In 1945 the family moved to Chiswick, west London, but unfortunately not long afterwards Vic's father died and his mother brought up the children on her own, which was not an easy task.

Vic's first job was as a delivery boy for Chandler's greengrocers, where he delivered around the local area to the homes of the rich and famous, which included Tommy Cooper, Jimmy Young, Adam Faith, Hugh Rynal and Shirley Bassey.

In 1959 Vic joined London Transport as a trolleybus conductor at Isleworth, but enlisted in the Army as a regular in 1961, where he became a corporal and met his future wife Anita, got married and had their family.

After being demobbed in 1967, Vic and his family moved to a two-roomed flat in Shepherds Bush and he rejoined London Transport as a driver after surviving the famous Chiswick skid pad!

With a third child on the way, Vic applied for a New Town transfer and, with a job at United Counties, moved to Huntingdon in 1968, where they remain today. Moving from a flat into a three-bed house with garden was a luxury. Vic was told by an old hand that it was on the cards that Huntingdon Depot would close shortly; however, 40 years later it is still operating, although it is likely to move, as the land is needed for housing.

Vic has always been a very active union man and after a number of years as a depot committee member he took over as the Union Branch Secretary for Huntingdon in 1980, becoming Branch Chairman in 1986. As a result of this appointment, he attended his first Central Consultative Committee meeting and became that Committee's Chairman in 1988. It was in this capacity that Vic led the workforce through the difficulties of privatisation, ensuring that no jobs were lost and that a pay increase was given each year, and the introduction of PRP (profit-related pay).

Another of Vic's jobs included being a trustee of the Pension Fund, and Workers Director for the Group ESOP (Employee Share Ownership Plan). Stagecoach had a 'buy one get one free' offer on shares, whereby the company doubled the number of any shares bought. Staff found this a good investment and still do at the time of writing.

When Stagecoach took over, Vic and a colleague from another subsidiary were instrumental in negotiating with Brian Souter and his team to get the best deal for the staff for pensions and related matters. Much of this work was done at Perth. These negotiations also resulted in no redundancies at Huntingdon.

By 1996 Vic had moved out of union work, leaving it to younger people, but he was willing and prepared to give advice on any union matters, especially agreements. By this time he was a Controller, still at Huntingdon.

Vic retired in January 2007 after 39 years with Huntingdon Depot. During his time there the number of vehicles increased from 12 to 44, and the workforce from 18 to 64, and the depot had been owned by United Counties, United Counties NBC, Stagecoach United Counties, Julian Peddle, Sovereign of Harrogate (with a local Head Office in Stevenage), Dennis Upton's Cavalier and finally, in May 2008, back to Stagecoach, but as Stagecoach in the Fens Ltd.

Huntingdon was a small but dedicated team, who worked together to provide the best bus service that resources would allow. Still working at Huntingdon at the time of writing are long-servers Terry Mead, as Operations Manager, engineer Paul Smith, Melvyn Karley, and Inspector John Cooper.

Ray Ramsey

Ray was seconded to Huntingdon in 1964 at the age of 18 to fill in for Inspector Jack Spicer while he was on sick leave. He remembers that Gerald Mead was then a conductor. He also remembers having to help count the takings every day with Mrs Girdwood, then take the cash to the bank in a bus and make up the wage packets. The telephone number was then Huntingdon 159, and when Ray picked up the receiver to make a call the operator used to say 'Good morning, Jack,' as it was Jack who usually made all the calls.

10
Irthlingborough Works

Ron Garon

Ron remembers that the works at Irthlingborough used to be on the right-hand side of the Finedon Road. The biggest house adjoining the works was for the Works Manager (Father Dean), and the next two were for the Inspectors. Next to the works was a row of three houses used for the Chief Engineer, Chief Inspector and Chief Bodyman. The final four houses were for Driver Eyres, Fitter Bill Coles, Mr and Mrs Garon and Ron, and Mr Dumain, a conductor.

Alfred Ernest Gibbs

Keith Gibbs tells us that his father Alfred worked as a bodybuilder in Irthlingborough Works from 1920, then transferred to Bedford Road Works in 1938. He died in 1949. Before working at Irthlingborough Alfred worked at Morgans and made Vimy bombers at Linslade. Each plane was pushed through the town to the park in order to attach the wings, then the planes took off from the park.

H. W. 'Tich' Hawes

Mr Hawes's memories have been supplied by Roger Warwick.

At the age of 14, after leaving Woodford Church of England School, on 20 April 1925 I started work at United Counties Bus Company at Irthlingborough. At that time this was the main works and Head Office. I cycled from home on roads that were very rough with plenty of small loose surface stones and potholes at regular intervals. It was a 5-mile journey to work through Great and Little Addington at 7.00am, six days a week. I had breakfast at 8.30-9.00am, lunch at

Irthlingborough Works, showing the houses in which Ron Garon was brought up. *Roger Warwick collection*

Alf Gibbs, Jack Craddock and Alf Griffin in the Body Shop at Irthlingborough. *Keith Gibbs collection*

1.00-2.00pm and clocked off at 5.30pm. On Saturdays we breakfasted at the same time and left work at 1.00 pm, giving us a total of 44½ hours a week.

I had to serve a seven-year apprenticeship to learn my bodybuilding trade but, unlike the present day, I did many other jobs, which would now be classed as labouring. Some of these jobs involved sweeping the benches and the shop floor, bagging the offcuts of wood, cleaning the machines and picking horsehair, which took up to a week and made my fingers quite sore by the time it was finished.

Another task I had to perform was painting under the bus body floors and under the top deck seats. The smell of the paint always gave me a bilious attack, yet despite its ill effects there was never any let-up. Another of my jobs was to go to the local shop for old cycle tubes. I stripped the tubes of any patches, cut them in half, then cut the whole length into half-inch strips, which were used for bedding the windows in the lower decks of all buses.

At this time there was an old unlicensed bus bearing the earlier name 'Wellingborough Omnibus Company'. There were 72 buses, which were all

Leylands and known as types A, B, C and S. We continued to build the S Type at Irthlingborough. They were constructed of wood: oak underframes, ash sides, Honduras mahogany panels, and deal tongue-and-groove boards fitted to both decks. The top decks were open, as were the stairs; on the top deck notices were displayed that warned passengers to lower their heads when going under bridges, and each seat carried a waterproof sheet in case of rain. The driver had what was called a scuttle panel, which came just above his waist. He sat on a long box seat under which was housed the petrol tank. Passengers were allowed to sit in front with the driver, and again a rain sheet was provided. The speed limit was 12mph, and the wheels were shod with solid rubber tyres. A few buses with electric lights were to be found, but many were still lit by carbide lamps. I would like to point out that at this period cycle lights were of a similar type. In the carbide lamps, water dripped at a controlled rate onto small greyish pieces of material (calcium carbide), which then gave off acetylene gas; this was piped to the head, tail and interior lower deck lights. The downstairs back rests and cushions were trimmed with

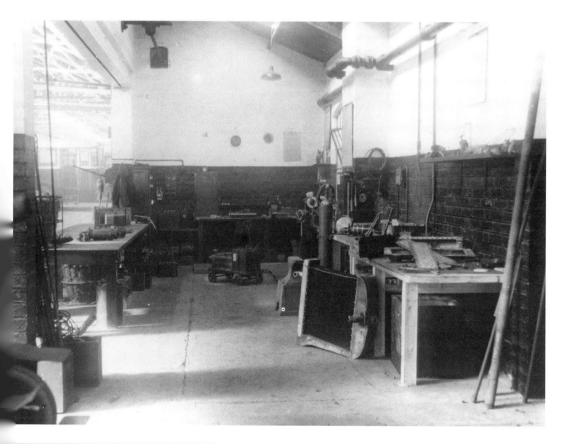

One of the shop areas at Irthlingborough. *Roger Warwick collection*

Alf Gibbs (extreme left) with colleagues including Richard ('Click') Taylor (extreme right). *Roger Warwick collection*

'Click' Taylor the bodyman. *John Appleton collection*

leather and filled with horsehair. All top deck seats and most in the lower deck were in pairs. The upper deck seats were made of slotted wooden slats, so that any water during rainstorms drained through them.

The completion of every new bus was quite an event. All maintenance staff were packed into the lower deck and asked to sway the body from side to side, then to bounce up and down with all their weight. As soon as these exercises proved satisfactory, the staff were then asked to fill all the seats upstairs and down. With this full-capacity load, the bus was then driven to Crow Hill, which was the steepest incline in the area, and given a climbing test.

At this stage the company was privately owned. One of the founders, Mr Thomas, died shortly before I started, but Mr Benjamin Richardson, the other owner, was very much alive. He lived in Kettering and at the back of his fairly large house there was a small garage that housed 13 vehicles. The owner and his son visited the works at regular intervals and his two daughters worked in an office to the right of the garage entrance, coming in from the Finedon Road. The office to the left housed a mixed bag including Father Dean, who was the Foreman Driver. He also made out the daily running sheet. Jim Moreton paid out the wages and I think Mr Pendred was also an early member of that group. Mr E. Bradford was the engineer in charge and Mr R. Smith was his office boy; another man, whose name I cannot remember, did the engineering drawing (his employment was short-lived). Mr G. Clark was in sole charge of the Body Shop, producing his own drawings and also doing all the buying for his department.

Woodworking machines were made by Wadkin and included a planer, circular saw and band saw. The lighting and power were supplied by two ex-Army searchlight engines.

The two quite large lamps with bulbs remained in the engine shop for some time. The dynamos produced 110 volts; they were only started when needed, using petrol, then, when they warmed up, paraffin. The blacksmith's forge had a hand-operated bellows.

The Paint Shop personnel were J. Craddock, W. Bardon, F. Mayes, C. Looms, J. Charles and W. Thomas; the latter two were labourers. A. Griffin, S. Hitchens, B. Nixon, A. Gibbs, J. Perkins and myself were the apprentices.

R. E. Taylor (nicknamed 'Click') was the wood machinist. Jack Perkins was our blacksmith and his striker was A. Ackers. Lastly, completing the Body Shop, A. Robinson looked after all the gas lighting. The engineering staff was comprised of T. Hayler (electrician), S. West, B. Coles, W. Wilkins, A. Green and B. Hoddle (these latter two were upgraded from the shop floor).

Engineering machine power was provided by a single-cylinder gas engine. This turned a very long shaft that went through the lathe shop and into the fitting department, where it also drove a pillar drill, a grindstone and a compressor, the latter being used to change the tyres. Rubber was bonded to steel bands and these were pressed on to cast-iron spoked wheels under very high pressure. Each machine had a free and fixed wheel; belts were moved at will by hand to start or stop them.

W. Tansley and S. Smith were the spring smith and striker. J. Wilmott kept the waste and carbide containers filled; he started his duties much earlier than the rest of the staff, owing to the fire risk, but despite this there was always a strong smell of acetylene gas when we arrived each morning. Our storeman, W. Grimes, left a short time after I started and emigrated to Canada; T. York then took over. W. Allen was the charge hand cleaner, W. Grimes's father was a cleaner and also Alf Soames.

There were four houses on each side of the garage entrance belonging to the company. In the first terrace Drivers H. Eyres and Garon occupied Nos 1 and 2, while B. Coles was in No 3 and conductor Hawkes in No 4, to the left. Living at No 1 in the right-hand terrace was T. Exma; when he died the house remained unoccupied until Bert Dean married some years later. G. Clark, J. Cox and E. Bradford occupied Nos 2, 3 and 4. J. Cox travelled daily on our service to Kettering, where he was Chief Inspector and stood at the library room where he directed traffic as and where needed. Indeed, in those days the only restriction a bus had was a licence plate to allow it to pick up passengers in the towns en route. There were also some stone cottages set at right angles to the latter terrace; J. Franklin, a local Inspector, J. Craddock and Father Dean, his daughter and Bert (Jack had already left home) lived in the larger of the three.

At the back of the garage there was a deep water pit into which all the rubbish was thrown, yet it never seemed to fill up. There was a small building at the front right-hand side of the garage housing two Napier cars that belonged to our Managing Director (one of them was later converted to a truck). He also owned two racehorses, one of which was called Iron Duke; I well remember the excitement in the workshops whenever they raced. Mr Richardson had by this time made United Counties a limited company. After his short illness and sudden death, which remains vividly in my mind, I recall how every bus carried a black crepe bow tied round its radiator cap.

I also noticed how quickly faces changed. The Misses Richardson and their brother left. Mr J. J. Johnson became the new Managing Director and his son and daughter soon appeared, the latter taking up duties in our Kettering Office. JJ (as he was always called by the men on the shop floor) also took over the Richardson's house. Father Dean now had another duty to perform as chauffeur to the new head, collecting him daily, taking him to the solicitors office and the Hind Hotel in Wellingborough, as well as the various offices of the company.

By this time my skills had been well taught and our new Director asked for various personal items to be made. Over a period of time I constructed a wheelbarrow, a henhouse and a dog kennel. I fitted a new back on the bureau and, with the aid of another craftsman, built a large summerhouse. As each item was completed, I received with much pleasure some appreciations, including a hobby drill, complete with case and 12 drills, a fretwork treadle machine, a jigsaw picture with base already prepared for cutting, and a chest for my woodworking tools, which I still have; whenever I was sent to the house I was always given a meal plus 2 shillings pocket money.

It was not long before we learned, with much regret, that body construction was to be phased out. The last body to be built was a single-decker on an old A Type chassis. This was unsuccessful because the lighter body bounced too much; the chassis had been fitted with pneumatic tyres, the speed increased and in consequence its life was very short. One other thing remains in my memory: plywood was invented at this time and was used for the very first time by us in this particular body. Everyone marvelled how it could be bent round corners without splitting. This was also the first vehicle to be steel-clad instead of having wooden panels. It was not very long before new buses began to arrive. The chassis was still manufactured by Leyland, all were fitted with the new type of tyres, and the D Type bodies were built by Christopher Dodson. At this time all the buses were converted to pneumatic tyres and screens were also fitted to the cabs, giving drivers much more comfort and protection.

As rolling stock increased, staff steadily grew with it. JJ became a man of wider interests when he started what later became known as the Nene Valley Sand & Gravel Company, and Mr J. Smith left our employ to become manager of this company. This in turn partially revived our Body Shop craft, because as old vehicles were scrapped we built tipper bodies on their chassis for this new enterprise.

Mr Hawes transferred to Bedford Road Works at Northampton when it opened, and retired in 1976 after 50 years service for the company. His last job was as Body Shop Superintendent.

Bernard Deacon and 'Tich' Hawes on the latter's retirement. *NBC News*

11
Kettering

Kettering was the major depot in the north of the county, with sub-depots and outstations at Corby, Desborough, Stamford and Thrapston.

Leonard Gentle

Once again, Mrs Birch has supplied the following information about her father. Leonard Gentle was transferred to Kettering in the mid-1960s, and was given a company car for the first time, moving to a private house at Higham Ferrers, where the

Kettering Depot from the air before the first bus station was built. *Roger Warwick collection*

Kettering's original bus station. *Roger Warwick collection*

The town's second bus station. The depot is on the left, with new housing on the right on the site of the old bus station. *Roger Warwick collection*

Leonard Gentle (extreme left) and some of his team at Kettering for Frank Ingram's retirement presentation. From left to right: Paul de Santis, Chris Brook-Taylor, Graham Coe, Charlie Sims, Corrie Smith, Margaret Ogilvie, Frank Ingram, Rose Hogan with Fido the dog, Ann, Vicky May, May Gardiner, Rachel Walker (Leonard Gentle's Secretary), Bill Cook, Dennis Noon, Douglas Cherry and Jack Hartley. *Mrs Birch collection*

In this retirement photograph Leonard Gentle (middle of the front row) is joined by friends including, in the back row, Colin Clubb, Bernard Routham, Tony Cassidy and Richard Christian. In the front row, left to right, are Charlie Carrington, Alan Crabbe, Madge Halton, Miss Cherry, Leonard Gentle, Mary Swanson, May Gardiner, Les Bidewell, Bill Smith Snr and Johnny Johnson. *Mrs Birch collection*

first Mrs Gentle died prematurely. Marrying again, Mr and Mrs Gentle moved to Irchester, then in 1979 to Warkton Lane in Kettering. Just before his second wife died, they moved to a bungalow in Desborough.

Leonard would not raise his voice often and was methodical in his thinking. He and his pipe would be seen contemplating on many an occasion. He did not mix socially with his other colleagues, except at company dinners and meetings; he felt that he could not admonish colleagues if he knew them socially. One colleague remembers that only after he came out of Mr Gentle's office did he realise that he had been told off. One day Leonard's pipe was hit and broke one of his teeth. This was a problem until he had a pipe-holding coat hanger made for him by the family.

Leonard was dedicated to United Counties and would be at work all the hours the job took. Many a dinner was spoiled, so after a while he would cook his own tea of bacon and eggs. To relax he used to retire to his shed to work on his carpentry. On retirement, the company bought him a mechanical saw, which was his pride and joy; his son-in-law now uses the same machine with pride.

Brian Mills was the Superintendent at Wellingborough before he went to the Rustenburg Bus Company in South Africa. After

settling in, he sent a letter to Len Gentle to thank him for all the help, training and assistance that Len and Norman Maycock had given him in attaining that new post. He went on to state that Len was a good friend and he hoped that one day he would be able to repay the friendship that he received from Len and his wife.

Tony Townsend

In 1977 Tony was appointed as Depot Engineer, based at Kettering and looking after the vehicles at Kettering, Corby, Stamford, Desborough and Thrapston. From those days he remembers that the chargehand at Corby was George Mair and that one of the cleaners was Brian Hadden. Ron Evans was

George and Grace Mair, Ernie and Mrs Smith, and the Townsend family. *Tony and Della Townsend collection*

the tyre fitter at Kettering and Mick Draper was a fitter. Marge Ord went to bingo with Tony's wife Della, Rita and Leonard Gentle, and Rachel Walker was Mr Gentle's Secretary. Bill Smith Jnr was also at Kettering.

In 1989, with the coming of privatisation, Tony retired from United Counties, and he and Della went off to drive and courier British and European tour coaches for two years, then worked on contracts for a firm in Desborough.

Gordon Smith

Gordon started his bus career in the East End of London, working out of Seven Kings Garage near Romford. His brother was working at Corby steelworks and in 1968 suggested Gordon come up to Kettering to drive. The house went up for sale and Gordon went to the depot in Northampton Road and asked Len Gentle for a job. He was taken on, but after six months the house had not sold, so Gordon was

Tony and his team had to rescue several buses in ditches. Two stricken Kettering vehicles are seen here ready for rescue. *Tony and Della Townsend collection*

forced to go back home. He worked for Grey-Green coaches for a year before moving back to Kettering with the family, after finally selling the house.

Len Gentle had no driving jobs so Gordon became a conductor. Eventually he became a driver again and worked at the depot until he retired in 1996.

Gordon remembers that his route-learning run included a trip to Stamford, which seemed to be a tour of the village hostelries. Gordon cannot remember the return to Kettering at all, as he did not drink much at that time and probably slept.

His first journey was to Thrapston, before any route learning – Gordon and Brian Pipe were 'going blind', as Brian was also new and had no idea of the area, but the passengers showed them where to go.

Gordon remembers that some shifts started at 4.15am to get the workers to Corby steelworks.

Spreadover shifts were worked where Gordon would work 5 hours and go home, then come back later and do 1½ hours. He remembers the standby shifts he did, when he wouldn't know whether he would get work until the normal driver failed to turn up.

One Sunday Gordon was reported for driving without due care and attention by a motorist who had let him out of the bus bay, then complained that Gordon had pulled out, blocking the road. As a result, Gordon was sent to Northampton for a retraining course, which lasted all day and consisted of many cups of tea, a trip 'on the cushions' to Northampton, a video, which was not relevant, and once round the test route.

On another occasion Gordon remembers a driver being accused of overtaking on a narrow bridge. This proved to be an unfounded allegation, but it affected

the driver so much that he had to retire on health grounds and died tragically as a result. Gordon and his colleagues were very upset by this incident, as drivers are very prone to being accused and are very often unable to answer back.

One day Gordon's mother-in-law was very poorly and he rang the garage to report that he was making an urgent visit to London; he could get no answer, but went off anyway. On his return he was called up to Len Gentle to explain himself. Apparently his bus was waiting up in the Bus Station for 4 hours before anyone missed him. The run was to Market Harborough, meeting up with another bus at Desborough. The whistle was blown when the other driver rang in and complained that no one had met him. Gordon was exonerated, and the Duty Inspector hauled over the coals for not noticing Gordon's

Gordon Smith (extreme right) with other long-serving staff in 1996. Back row (left to right): Richard Oakley, Neil Forsyth, Sidney Lovett, Kevin O'Leary, Reginald Hillyard, Richard Scholes, Bill Nicholson, Lyn Worboys, Brian Barton, Peter Rayner, Bernard Tear, Malcolm Howitt and Tony Cox. Front row: Bill Smith Jnr, Douglas Graham, Harold Barnes, Jeannie Warwick, Peter Ward, Graham Coe, Nicholas Egan and Patrick Mustin. *Gordon Smith collection*

absence.

Gordon remembers one driver who suffered from a sleeping disorder, and was taken off driving until he was brought back to stability with pills. However, the conductor could tell when he was asleep, as the bus hit the kerb; ringing the bell would wake the driver up, and off they would go again. Another driver was reputed to have worked with 18 pints inside him – he worked on automatic pilot that day.

Kettering's Social Club did not have a venue and used to meet at various pubs and clubs. Most club events were informal and very enjoyable.

Gordon compiled a list of his colleagues and remembers that the driving instructors were Brian Barton and Fred Hooton.

George Hawkins

George Hawkins spent six weeks of his road service as a conductor at Kettering and Corby. He remembers that at Corby fares were charged at the conductors' discretion, 10p for some and 20p for others. He did not know

The Church of St. Mary Magdalene
Geddington

"Family Man"

BRIAN RALPH BARTON

10TH JULY 1941 - 22ND OCTOBER 2005

"CELEBRATING A VERY SPECIAL LIFE"

Wednesday 2nd November 2005

Instructor Brian Barton as all his colleagues remember him. *Brian Hadden and the Kettering team*

Kettering conductors count their day's takings. *Roger Warwick collection* the prices or the fare stages, and took what he was given. One duty he remembers was when working the town services at Corby. One way was the 285 and the other way the 286; one bus was a Kettering crew and bus while the other was a Corby bus with a Kettering crew. The former crew would pick up the latter crew at the depot if they arrived before them, otherwise the second crew would have to walk back to Kettering. This meant a rush round the route, dump-parking the bus at Corby Depot and running to the bus stop.

There was only a mess room at Corby and no canteen. The latter was provided at the steelworks, and canteen staff from Kettering drove out there to provide breakfast between 05.45 and 06.15, and lunch at 13.45 to 14.15. Supper at 21.45 to 22.15 was tea or coffee only. The staff bus driver would be used as a staff bus in the works when not needed otherwise.

The first sign-on at Kettering was at 04.20, compared to Luton at 05.05, and the last one in was at 23.50.

Graham Coe

Graham has been working at Kettering Depot since he joined United Counties in 1961. He has moved from one desk to another, but apart from that he has been in the same office.

He started as the Setright clerk. These ticket machines were kept in lockers and Graham's job was to record the number on the waybill, which was then checked for accuracy. Graham worked with Jack Gilbert in those days.

Later he worked as the Outstation Detailer, covering rotas with spaces due to holidays or sickness. This could be a nightmare at times. His next job was as Assistant to the Depot Manager, Len Gentle – although in those days it was Leonard Gentle. Graham was a detailer and is now a wages clerk, working two days a week.

The conductors' lockers at Kettering. They had doors at each end so that conductors could put their boxes in and the office staff could remove them to check the waybills. *Roger Warwick collection*

Maureen Draper (née Johnson)

Maureen lived with her parents in Geddington and used to travel into Kettering daily. Her second job after school was working at Kettering Depot, where she worked for a few years before marrying a soldier and moving away. Her first task was to make the tea. Mr Gentle was her boss and one day she was admonished for being late, but on being summoned by Mr Gentle she was sent on her way. Her boss, Margaret Ogilvie, was admonished instead.

During her stay with United Counties Maureen was the receptionist, cashier and enquiry clerk, and did

Graham Coe in his original chair. *Brian Hadden collection*

some days at Corby Bus Station and in the canteen. When she was a cashier she remembers that 99% of the cash was no problem, but several conductors/drivers had to be chased up. When the money was cashed it was loaded on to the spare bus and driven up to the Midland Bank, where it parked in the middle of the road, blocking the street. Maureen had a crew assigned to her as escort. She remembers the other girls in the office, Chrissi Roe and Paula.

The wage cheque with reconciliation was sent down from Northampton weekly on the bus, and this involved another trip to the bank on the spare bus. This time she collected the money, which was then counted out and put into envelopes. One day they were a 50p coin short, and all the envelopes were reopened, checked and resealed. Five hundred envelopes were done at Kettering for Corby, Desborough, Thrapston and Stamford. Desborough had a staff of 20 and Thrapston had four crew members.

Any bookings in the enquiry office for Associated Motorways were passed to Northampton, then to Cheltenham.

It was during her time at Kettering that Maureen first met Mick Draper, whom she married many years later.

Ted Wittering's retirement: left to right are Terry Oram, Ted, Fred Moisey, George Millen, Ernie Vincent, Maureen Draper and Rance Muskett. *Mick and Maureen Draper collection*

at Kettering were Cyril Smith, Doug Cherry, Charlie Carrington and Bill Herbert. He also remembers Sid Webster (Superintendent), Harold Olchin, Wilf Johnson and 'Pop' Mayo (Body/Paint Shop man) in 1957.

Mick Draper

Mick started work at Kettering Garage in 1954 and retired 33¾ years later. After his apprenticeship, he worked mainly in the depot engineering side and did occasional driving at weekends and when required.

One day one of the Inspectors had been very offhand with someone, so the fitters arranged for a bus to block his car in; they took the wheels off the bus, then went to lunch. Instead of going home at 1.00pm, the Inspector was kept there until 2.30. All except the Inspector were satisfied with this, as he was off on two weeks' holiday and was rushing home to pack! The Inspectors

Anthony Italiano, George Davis and Mick Draper at Kettering Depot. *Mick and Maureen Draper collection*

Mick was part of the breakdown crew and remembers the tragic road deaths of two of his driving colleagues. He attended one and still remembers it now. He also remembers sadly that a colleague Ron Wesley died in a car crash. Each death had a great effect on the staff at Kettering.

Mick remembers the breakdown truck, GKU 744, with affection. Under trade plate 125 BD, he drove it many times. He also drove many crippled vehicles to the main works at Northampton. One day he was driving a bus that needed a new radiator after an accident, and had to stop to keep filling it up. He was accosted by an Inspector, who sent for the tow truck to pull the bus back in. However, Mick had filled up and was at Bedford Road before the tow truck had left.

Kettering's LS buses were known as 'trams' and the first Lodekka, which arrived on 1 August 1955, was nicknamed 'Scharnhorst' after the German battleship sunk in December 1943. Talking of the war, Mick remembers the Air Raid Shelter at the back of the building. Kettering had the last four UCOC KSWs, KNV 338-341.

The first year he worked at Kettering Mick was given one week's holiday, which was a bonus for him, never having had one before.

Leonard Gentle was affectionately known as 'Harry Worth' by his team, due to his nature and his glasses; Harry Worth was a bumbling, bespectacled comedy actor popular on TV during the 1960s. Mr Gentle's company car was a blue Ford Escort, registration MNH 645H.

Mick had a reputation for being a 'squirrel' for stores. When Johnny Johnson was at Bedford Road Works he only had to ring and the item was on a truck at once; Mick had a lot of respect for Johnny, and knew he would get the item back. Mick was so well known that he would go to Northampton Stores and help himself, only seeing the Storeman when he was ready to go.

Lots of couples got together at Kettering Depot. Mick and Maureen were one, and they remember at least four others. They are still friends with Mary Rowney who worked in the depot with her husband George, Mary as a conductress and George as an electrician.

Nick Egan at London Zoo in 1976. *Author's collection*

Nick Egan

Nick joined the company in 1961 as a conductor; he later moved to driving, then became the Engineering Supervisor. His present post is as the depot shunter.

He remembers one trip to Northampton vividly, when he was 'strafed' by a plane near the Red House. The plane crashed into a field, and Nick ran over to find the RAF pilot with a head wound. He rang the emergency services and waited for them to arrive. On reaching Northampton Bus Station he was reprimanded for being late and lost pay as a result on returning to Kettering (also late). This incident appeared in the *Evening Telegraph*.

Fred Moore

Fred started at Welford as a conductor during 1964-66. He still has a wallet containing his request to attend for an interview at Derngate by Superintendent Maycock.

He transferred to Kettering as a driver, then a coach driver and controller for National Express, then Stagecoach. He left in December 2005 and is

Nick Egan having a well-earned break at Kettering Depot. *Brian Hadden collection*

now a coach driver for an independent coach firm. He found the transfer to Kettering something of a cultural change, and had to do as he was told instead of thinking for himself. He joined the union, as he could not work at Kettering without being a member. He also joined the staff welfare organisation, which has since been wound up.

Fred remembers that a bus was sent to Stamford weekly with the company wages and the crew came back 'on the cushions' to Corby, then Kettering. At Kettering there were 15 office staff, including four Inspectors. Len Gentle was in charge of the depot and was a real gentleman. At Wellingborough the team included Jeff Manning, who was in charge in 1966, with Mr McRoberts as Depot Manager, Inspector Brown and Ernie Barrett.

LWL 427 was the depot's pet bus, which was used for trips to events. On a trip to Crich Tramway Museum with Bristol MW GRP 262D, Fred drove part of the way and impressed Mr Gentle. Drivers had to have two years' experience before driving coaches and Fred was one of the youngest.

Kettering was an important coaching depot, the main routes served being Cheltenham to Peterborough/Kings Lynn/Boston and Corby to London. Summer services were Corby to Eastbourne; Desborough to Yarmouth; reliefs to Cheltenham, Weymouth and back to Northampton; and Northampton to Portsmouth (jointly with Royal Blue). At times of shortages, coaches were hired from Hants & Dorset, Southern Vectis and Trent.

Father Christmas Fred Moore on his way to Kettering Bus Station with the toys. *Tony and Della Townsend collection*

In the summer eight or nine coaches would go to Cheltenham. On Fred's first journey, a customer thought he was very good for taking the cases and collecting the tickets on behalf of the driver; he was very surprised when he found he was actually talking to the driver. At Cheltenham, the Black & White Inspectors were feared, including Len Williams, Bob Sugar, Joe Jackson, Tony Leddington and Jim Smith. One of Fred's favourite coaches was former Birch Brothers 195, as it drove well and was quick.

Fred was a union man and was involved in a strike when the company decided to single-man the bus to Aberdeen. Milton Keynes drivers did the job when Kettering refused; one day the bus went up to Edinburgh (driver change), and next day it returned. When it got to Kettering the bus was barricaded in by staff and was unable to continue. After making their protest they allowed the bus to leave.

One day during a strike a relief crew were given chocolate by a passenger. Apparently it was the laxative Exlax, and the crew were in need of the loo more often!

Part of Fred's union training was a Health & Safety course at Coventry. This included not only the Act itself but COSH and environmental rules. One day Fred was asked to copy the Stagecoach risk assessment for the company; he was on a spare turn that day and it gave him something to do. He did it six times, four for the company, one for him and one for a friend. This was then used in future dealings with the management.

While in the rest room at Cheltenham, drivers were summoned by Tannoy. Fred was admonished one day for not jumping to the Inspector's tune straight away. As a punishment, he was sent back home via Stratford-upon-Avon and Coventry. Fortunately, the coach was not needed after Coventry and Fred was sent home direct (going via his parents' home at Lutterworth).

Coach drivers working overtime were paid an extra 3 hours if more than a minute over; at weekends the extra 3 hours was paid at time and a half.

Two Kettering drivers were killed on duty. Dave Wardle was driving a Bedford single-decker on the 407/8 from Wellingborough in 1976. The temperature was hot and the tar had melted by the Harrowden turn. A cattle wagon skidded on the wet, smooth road and hit the bus sideways. Eric Taylor was killed while driving a Bristol RELH on the M1; apparently he collided with a stationary road tanker.

Fred also remembers that on coaching turns the drivers used to get perks on the ferries and at venues visited. Unfortunately the management team got to hear about these and they were stopped. Fred recalls that some drivers used to be very friendly with their passengers and others were miserable – Fred was one of the friendly ones. He used to be one for the ladies, and one day he was going upstairs to chat one up. An Inspector got on and caught him, but fortunately

Fred is driving a preserved LWL bus with Tim Roberts and friend Bruce McCormack. *Kettering Evening Telegraph*

he was not reprimanded too strongly for his actions. Some conductors were sacked for being friendly with female passengers.

Mary Rowney

I was a clippie for 35 years at Kettering Depot. I started in 1944, while the war was still on. Everyone had to be registered for some war work at the age of 18, and I was sent to work on the buses.

This job was a very cold job in the winter with open-backed double-deckers and no heating. I remember going through the terrible winter of 1947 with buses getting stuck in snowdrifts quite frequently.

We clippies had to climb up on the front of the bus to change the destination blinds by hand. Our earliest start was 4.45am and the latest finish was at midnight, because we had to take the workers to the steelworks at Corby ready for their shifts. We had a different driver every week, so if we didn't get on too well we just had a week with him!

When the war ended in 1945 I could have left, but I was used to the job and liked it, so I stayed on. If you did your job properly there was no one bossing you about compared with factories with foremen.

I met my husband at the bus garage, when he came out of the RAF and worked as an electrician to keep the buses working.

Eventually I took early retirement

George and Mary Rowney. *Mick and Maureen Draper collection*

in 1980, as the buses were all going to one-person-operation, so we clippies and the conductors became surplus to requirements. I missed it terribly at first, but got use to being a housewife. My husband retired from UCOC at the age of 65 and we had a short retirement together before he was sadly diagnosed with Alzheimer's disease in 2001. He passed away in 2006. I am now 81 and living on my own, but with some happy memories.

TGWU Kettering, 1948-54

During those years the union was involved in raising money for employees on long-term sick leave (after 12 weeks), the money being raised by raffles. There was also a benevolent fund and a fund for looking after poor children (£26). In 1949 the union raised a total of £238 4s 4d.

Other matters in which the union became involved were:
* The Kettering Trades Council
* Views on the employment of drivers direct from outside, instead of through the ranks of conductors
* Long hours worked due to shortage of staff
* Condition of company vehicles
* New uniforms and smocks (for the summer)
* Members' disciplinary hearings by management
* Workers' buses to Rothwell and Burton Latimer
* Allocation of routes between depots (the Rothwell dance bus and Corby services)
* Timings for routes, for example that to Leicester
* Setright ticket machines, which could not be read at night
* Alterations to bus stops for the health and safety of company employees and customers
* The Wicksteed bus from the station
* 'Buses turning' signs for the entrance and exit of the garage
* Private hire being given to senior members of the committee in preference to others, which was shown to be false information.

The TGWU logo on Kettering's list of members.

From the Kettering Archive

Lesley, Adrian and Alan

Colin and Elanda Reed with Jim Webb, Brian Laywood, Brian Hadden and Michelle Hargreaves.

John and Victoria Letch

Gill McAlwane

Dave Gobbett

Steven Ogden

Inglis Lyon, Brian Hadden and Bob Montgomery

Paddy Mustin

Mick Dodds, Fred Moore, Gordon Chenery, Shaun Starkey and John ? with their partners at the retired members dinner in 2006.

Barry Hinde and Graham Coe (sitting)

Nick Shipton (right)

Lenny Stolarski

Unknown crew members in Kettering Bus Station. *Alan Parfitt collection*

A bus outside the Library in Kettering. *Alan Parfitt collection*

Gordon Smith and Les Bayes. *Mick Hedge collection*

Glen Harvey, Kim Chambers, Simon Mobbs, Roger Smith and Steve Swannell

12
Leighton Buzzard

Leighton Buzzard outstation. *Roger Warwick collection*

Leighton Buzzard was an outstation for Luton.

Roy Stone and George Hawkins

Roy Stone used to drive at Leighton Buzzard, then Dunstable, with his brother Roger. Roy drove for 39 years and Roger 36 years. Roy remembers that Wally White was the oldest driver, having started in 1921 and finishing in 1965.

Leighton Buzzard had 16 drivers and 16 conductors. George Hawkins adds that the depot was the largest outstation with ten vehicles – nine double-decker buses and one single-decker – and was owned by a car repair business; it therefore had to be cleared of buses during the day, and no buses were allowed in until after tea time. Although out of bounds during the day, the paying-in room at the back was open all day. The day's takings were individually put into the night safe at the Midland Bank in Leighton Buzzard. Leighton had no allocated engineering staff and an Inspector ran the depot.

All rotas were designed so that staff had their meal breaks at Luton. The vehicles were also fuelled and changed during these breaks.

Local paper shops used to sell United Counties weekly tickets.

13
Luton

United Counties had a bus garage in Castle Street, and this depot had the largest number of buses in the United Counties fleet. It also had the largest complement of staff to cover the depot's work. Luton had a sub-depot at Hitchin and an outstation at Leighton Buzzard.

Over the years there have been three bus stations in Luton. The original was behind the library and had 15 bays (the same as at Kettering), the second in front of the library and the third underneath a multi-storey car park in Bute Street, on the site of the old railway

line to Dunstable. This is now closed and buses pick up in the streets around the area.

Buses were allocated routes due to many factors. Low bridges meant single-deckers, and narrow streets with 90-degree bends meant shorter vehicles. Newer buses worked the country routes, while the 'old crocks' plodded round the town services. Some buses were high-bridge vehicles, and had plaques in the cabs to notify drivers of the fact. The oldest buses worked on the 56 route to Runfold, which ran every 5 minutes. Most crews stayed together for long periods of time.

Luton Depot. *Roger Warwick collection.*

The main impression at Luton was that, being remote from the Head Office in Northampton, it always received the cast-offs from other depots and companies. Northampton being in the Western Area, and Luton in the Eastern Area, meant that the depots in each area rarely cooperated together. Socially the staff visited more depots in each area than at work, and Luton staff used to have great Christmas parties.

Luton also felt that it was a poor relation with the allocation of coaches. When Bristol MW 134 was involved in an accident on the Barnet Bypass, the mileage was 1,000 miles per week and the total was very high.

Luton controlled the sub-depot at Leighton Buzzard, and had an outstation at Clophill for a short time before returning it to Bedford. Clophill housed two Bristol KSWs, 945 and 969, in those days.

The Eastern National Superintendent was Mr Kershaw and Mr Buckmaster was the District Traffic Superintendent. In these days Luton had two Bristol L coaches numbered 352 and 354. Mr Crew was the Traffic Manager and the Depot Superintendent was Bob Rumbold, who had arrived from Hitchin in 1956. At Hitchin he was replaced by a Mr Kenyon. Mr Rumbold's badge of authority was always his bowler hat. Wakes weeks started in mid-July, which caused a lack of staff at United Counties. Conversely, coaches and some dual-purpose vehicles were delicensed in the winter, and Castle Street bus park was then full.

At Luton there were four types of road staff rotas: (a) town work only, including four runs to Leagrave on the 54/57 routes and after lunch four more, or four runs to Sundon Park, lunch and four more on services 50, 51 and 52; (b) town and country work; (c) spreadover duties for experienced staff (this had a waiting list); and (d) OMO rotas.

John Horn was the Body Shop Foreman when the Luton operation was sold to Luton & District in 1986. Roy Witherspoon was the shift fitter, and as

The office windows were unusual in having rounded tops. This office had two rows of desks, with the Wages Office in a separate section.
Mrs Birch collection

vehicles sometimes ran out of fuel on Saturday nights he would substitute freshly fuelled vehicles at Saturday teatime to save him going out to vehicles running out of fuel. Norman Mitchell was the Supervisor at Bedford Road Depot in Northampton.

When the first Bristol LDs – 950, 951 and 952 – came to Luton they were used on the Leagrave services.

Eric Miles was a top coach driver and his favourite steed was Bristol LS 439; they usually worked the Bournemouth run. His conductor was named

Donaldson, who later became an Inspector after much encouragement. LS 440 was mainly used on the Margate run. After 439 Eric was allocated 468, a six-cylinder bus. Eric also had 117, also a Bristol LS, which stayed at Luton for most of its career.

Mr Cooksley was the driver of the Portsmouth Express coach, service X24, and Pat Murphy drove the Eastbourne coach, Bristol LS 460. The Clacton coach was service X32 and the Yarmouth coach was numbered 486.

Excursions were also run from Luton, and Bristol LSs 481 and 482 were reduced to 35-seaters for this work, although this was short-lived. To replace them new coaches 114 and 115 were allocated. Replacements again came in the form of 200-203. However, when the excursions ceased 114, 115, 200, 201 and 202 were all sold on; 203 stayed on to be the Directors' coach and finished up in National Travel livery. In departmental days it became a uniform store.

Offley Hill was very steep, and in the winter it could be a problem to get up it in snow and ice. Five-cylinder buses used to go up in first gear at 5mph, while a Bristol LS with 41 customers and luggage did it at 3mph.

Aylesbury was the first depot to go to one-person-operation in a big way; others were slower due to union resistance. The vehicles used were Bristol LSs in the 100+ series. Its Bristol LDs – 971, 991, 996 and 998 – were the best maintained.

Alan Parfitt

Alan is a life-long bus enthusiast who worked for United Counties during summer vacations in the late 1950s and early 1960s. During his time with the company he helped to organise the summer express services that in those days took holidaymakers from Luton to such exotic destinations as Bournemouth, Yarmouth and Clacton. He also helped with other traffic duties. Alan retains an involvement in buses as part-owner of former United Counties Bristol FS6G KBD 712D, and through the Herts & Beds Group of the Omnibus Society.

The offices at Luton were at one side of the garage and overlooked Castle Street. The ground floor housed the cash and ticket offices and the conductors' paying-in room. Upstairs was the office of Mr Rumbold, the District Traffic Superintendent, the Wages Office staffed by Mrs McCann and Sally, and the General Office.

Some of the Luton staff at Castle Street, including Mr Donaldson, A. Thomas, Tom Edison, Jack King, 'Curly' Rolf, Mr Rumbold, Norman Midgley, Frank Gatehouse, Jack Kinsellor and Johnny Johnson. *EFE Showbus Gallery*

Luton Depot extension and new offices, with Colin Clubb, Michael Carr and Ernie Smith at Luton. The gentleman with the bow-tie is the Mayor of Luton and the lady is his Secretary. *Colin Clubb collection*

Those whom Alan remembers from the General Office are Mrs Harrison and later Mrs Coates, who organised the coaching activities, which included private hire and excursions. Mrs Meek was one of those charting for the express services and also handling lost property. Mrs Newman was the receptionist and operated the main telephone switchboard. Also remembered was Janet, who joined as a copy-typist but stayed with the company and its successors, later becoming Graham Cumming's Personal Assistant when he was Managing Director of Luton & District.

The maintenance staff had their own office, adjoining the dock area, and were headed by Mechanical Superintendent Frank Gatehouse.

Bookings for the summer coastal express services were made either at the main company enquiry office or at one of many agents in shops around the district. The main enquiry and booking office was initially in Park Street, run by Mrs Kendal. It later moved to a joint office with Luton Corporation Transport in Bute Street.

Details of bookings were passed to the office at Castle Street and recorded on charts. They were then sorted into coach loads and vehicles allocated. These were either the company's own, such as Bristol LS5G 439 and 440, Bristol LS6Bs such as 468, 469, 470 and 471, or hired-in vehicles. Subsequently Luton received some more modern coaches such as Bristol LS6G 117, Bristol MW6Gs 140 and 150, and later Bristol RELH6Gs 252 and 264.

It was always a bone of contention that Luton only received older coaches, usually cascaded from Northampton and having been well used on London-Motorway-Northampton-Leicester-Nottingham services. For peak Saturdays extensive use was made of hired-in coaches to provide duplicates; among the many operators used included Simmonds of Letchworth, Taylor's Reliance of Meppershall, Red Rover from Aylesbury.

Saturdays during Vauxhall Motors' holiday weeks could see more than 100 coaches leaving Castle Street at 7.45am. Alan's 21st birthday treat was to travel as a passenger to Bournemouth on Bristol LS6B 468 in the capable hands of Eric Miles. Eric was the company's leading driver in Luton. On arrival it was time for a quick bite to eat, then help to load the dozen or so coaches for the return journey.

When the summer peak was past, Alan helped with other traffic tasks around the office. These

Barbara Meek (second row, left) and her colleagues at Luton. *Mrs Birch collection*

buses. However, unlike Northampton, the Luton agreement extended to a full sharing of both mileage and revenue on a 50-50 basis within the coordination area, which included not only Luton and Dunstable but also more rural areas such as Toddington and Whipsnade.

At that time the Luton/Dunstable area was still growing, with new estates such as Tithe Farm at Houghton Regis for the London Overspill, so there was a continuing need for new services and more buses. In contrast, even in those days evening loadings were declining, leading to frequent reductions. Out of town work included runs to Aylesbury, Toddington (where there was a small two-bus outstation) and Leighton Buzzard, which had a larger outstation of about ten buses. To the east, operation of the money-spinning 52 or later 92 group of routes out to Letchworth, Baldock and Stotfold was shared with Hitchin Depot.

Leighton Buzzard mainly worked the services to Luton, but put one bus on the Aylesbury to Bedford service (141). Later the 141 service was linked with the Bedford to St Ives route, with a journey time of some 4 hours end to end. The vehicles on this route had often started in the morning at a different depot, meaning that vehicles could easily get lost for days when engineering staff were chasing them for routine servicing. In contrast, crews generally wished to return to their homes at night, leading to some strange duty instructions such as 'Proceed from Bedford towards Aylesbury until meeting the bus coming the other way and swap'. This worked fine unless one bus was running late! Vehicles allocated to this route were Bristol LDs numbered 544, 545 and 546.

Unusually, Luton regularly used six-cylinder vehicles on town services. Most depots used only the five-cylinder 'potters'. Alan's favourites were the Bristol KSW6Bs, robust and indestructible; they took all that the harsh conditions, hills and heavy loads of Luton threw at them. Particular favourites were a batch of four – 895, 896, 897 and 898 – which spent most of their time on service 8 (later 28) between Round Green and Farley Hill.

Corby, where the town services were tightly timed,

included checking loading figures, new fare tables and even some amateur scheduling. One interesting task was the delivery of the previous day's takings to the bank, usually using the training bus (No 3, a pre-war Bristol L5G). Parked at George Street, Alan helped carry the bags of coins into the bank; no one would ever steal them, as they were far too heavy! On wages days Mr Rumbold and Chief Inspector Davy would go to the bank in the little Austin A35 staff car and bring back the cash, protected only by a wooden cosh, just in case. The Wages Office was then locked while the team assembled the wage packets for distribution in the garage.

On the bus side, most of Luton's work was town services. As in Northampton, a coordination agreement had been made with the Corporation

The Park Street offices. *Mrs Birch collection*

was the only other depot at that time to similarly use six-cylinder buses around town. Bedford services in the late 1950s were operated by a motley collection of elderly Bristol K5Gs and L5Gs. If for any reason a Lodekka found its way into the town, it was removed as soon as possible. This situation was turned on its head when Kenneth Wellman took over as Traffic Manager. He argued that it was the town services that provided most of the money, and introduced brand-new Bristol FS6Bs, with electric platform doors, to the main cross-town route.

Castle Depot was a lively place in those days. The allocation was mainly double-deckers. Single-deckers found little use except on the service 66 to Bletchley and 14 to Barton and Shefford. These services were some of the first from Luton to be one-man-operated (OMO) using two Bristol LS saloons, 480 (an LS6B 'flyer') and 450 (an LS5G 'crawler'). The latter retained its coach seating and was often required for express duty on peak Saturdays, so it was then necessary to substitute a crewed double-decker on the OMO workings. However, at Bletchley, due to the low

railway bridge, such workings had to turn short of the railway station. 'Captain' Brown was one of the first OMO drivers.

Luton also provided breakdown cover for coaches on the M1 motorway between Scratchwood Services and Newport Pagnell Services. The night-shift fitters were often called out, and arriving at Castle Street in the morning one might see a Standerwick Leyland Atlantean or a Bristol VRLL coach standing forlornly in the corner of the yard awaiting attention.

Among the Inspectors, Alan remembers Jack Pirton. He was not always the most smartly presented Inspector but he had grown up in London and had an encyclopaedic knowledge of both the general and the pirate bus operations in the capital. Jack was also an avid collector of bus tickets, many dating from the early part of the 20th century.

Turnover of staff at Luton was very high due to the higher wages paid at Vauxhall Motors and other factories. There was an agreement that the Corporation would not poach United Counties staff and vice versa. However, the Corporation Transport paid higher rates and gave pensions and other fringe benefits.

In 1970 United Counties acquired the Corporation buses. Some of the vehicles, such as the Bristol RELLs, fitted well into the merged fleet, although the first batch (361-369) were not popular because of their manual gearboxes. The Leyland and Dennis double-deckers did not fare so well and had only short lives with United Counties, being replaced with a varied assortment of elderly Bristol Lodekkas from other Tilling companies. Some of the most popular of these were those from Red & White Services, with six-cylinder Gardner engines and five-speed gearboxes – speedy machines! Others were less favourably received.

Following the break-up of United Counties in 1986, Alan followed the fortunes of the newly established Luton & District under the direction of Stan Morris and later Graham Cumming. These were exciting days with the development of minibus operations under the 'Hopperstopper' label and the acquisition of Red Rover at Aylesbury and later of London Country North West. Going private in 1987, the company was sold to the Cowie Group, which later became Arriva Shires & Essex. Castle Street Garage has now been demolished and a Matalan store stands on the site. The Arriva depot is now at 487 Dunstable Road.

Alan went on to University to pursue a career in the Civil Service.

Alan and Christine Parfitt aboard Bristol FS 712 on their wedding day in 2008. *Alan and Christine Parfitt collection*

George Hawkings

George worked for United Counties from 1959 to 1974. As already mentioned, Luton had three bus garages, for Luton Corporation, United Counties and London Transport. London Transport could only work to the south, by agreement, while Luton Corporation and United Counties had agreements and joint services. In 1970 this was an advantage when the two merged. Both companies were always short of staff, with competition from Vauxhall Cars, Commer Trucks and Skefco.

Some staff worked for life, while others were in and out quickly. The workforce was made up of about one-third local people, one-third from the Caribbean and Asia and one-third from Ireland. In later days many staff transferred from London Transport as they were promised new houses in the London Overspill areas of Luton and Aylesbury. Some of the Irish were living six to a room and had all their meals at the bus depot. They were all good workers and only went on strike once when one of the Inspectors said something he should not have done about the Pope when a driver on the 05.30 spare turn with a 12.30 finish would not work a run finishing at 12.32 as he had to go to church.

The odd bus was outstationed at Dunstable in Williamson Street. These were usually used for the

Luton Depot workshop area. *Roger Warwick collection*

staff buses, as Len Bright, one of the drivers, lived at Dunstable. The four drivers there were all OMO drivers, and the buses collected and dropped United Counties and Luton Corporation staff and postmen. Len Bright's father ran a small coach business running from Dunstable to Edlesborough. This service was taken over by Eastern National and Len was taken over as well, being given a job for life.

For a short time Bletchley also came under the control of Luton. The foreman was Albert Lambert, and the road crew contact was the toilet attendant at the bus station. Bletchley reverted to Stony Stratford after a short time. On one visit Mr Rumbold left his trademark bowler hat behind, and after an urgent phone call it was sent back to Luton on the next bus. Legend has it that the bus arrived at Luton Bus Station with the driver wearing the bowler hat to the merriment of his colleagues.

George and his family lived in Slip End, on a London Transport route. He remembers that Dunstable to Luton was a joint route with Luton Corporation with a bus every 5 minutes. All buses were packed with passengers. The 06.30 Aylesbury to Luton working had to be duplicated from Dunstable to Luton and back to Aylesbury.

George was thrown off the bus once when he

mimicked the Welsh conductor, and had to walk. This conductor was from Aylesbury and later they had a laugh when George became his boss.

The United Counties garage had its entrance in Castle Street and its exit in Chapel Street, being located between the two streets. George remembers that the Wages Office became his office when he returned as manager. In the early years he was at the desk in the corner of the Main Office. The wages clerks were Sally Lovell and Mrs McCann, and Sally's sister Ann worked as a typist. One day all office work ceased when the Queen drove past – this was the highlight of the day.

George's father Fred was a driver and Inspector at Luton Corporation Transport, so George followed his father into the business, being recommended by Corporation managers. He was offered a traineeship by Donald Crew at Luton. Fred joined the Corporation to get a pension, and worked with conductress Jenny Edmonds. George became a company trainee in 1959, going to Northampton for one year then to Luton as the odd job boy in the office. By 1964 he had become the Depot Manager at Aylesbury, taking over from Leonard Gentle and staying until 1970, when he was promoted to Depot Manager at Luton. In 1972 promotion came again

George Hawkins. *NBC News*

However, at Northampton the drivers went down the rota one place every week and the conductors up one. This meant that driver and conductor would only be on the same roster every two years, and each thus needed to tolerate the other for just a week.

Other staff remembered by George are driver and union convenor Eric Miles, Driving Instructors Reg Barnard and Wally Batts, and driver Fred Bass and his wife Lily, who was a conductress. Another character at Luton, known by father and son, was 'Captain' Brown, who was reported to have been a hero in the Army. By the time George knew him he was retired but still working, filling the bus radiators with water.

Driver Lewin Brown was also a character. He worked regularly with conductress Ivy Joslyn, and one year they went on holiday together to America and had a good time. When asked why he had not taken his wife, he stated that he had taken her to Bognor Regis for a week earlier on and that was all she was to expect! Bill Catt was another driver, and driver Eddie Costain would rather work than go home, and was always dressed immaculately. Another immaculate dresser was driver Jack King, who became a clerk due to ill health. Inspector Edmunds came over from the Corporation, and Evelyn Grave was another conductress. Father and son Cole worked at the depot; father was known as 'Pop' and son as 'Sonny'.

George remembers an incident when the brakes failed on a former Corporation Dennis Loline when going down a very steep hill. To stop the bus the driver went through the wall of the cemetery on the bend, halfway down. Unfortunately he suffered delayed shock and a couple of days later he finished his shift, then collapsed and died by his front door.

The service to Aylesbury always had the best buses allocated as this was the showcase route from Luton. Bristol Lodekkas 993, 994 and 995 were used when new, followed by Bristol FLFs 617, 618, 619 and 620.

The 09.15 bus out of Luton, 'the fisherman's', on a Sunday had to be duplicated, usually to 1½ busloads, as Ivinghoe was a great destination for fishing. On Sundays and Bank Holidays special buses went to Dunstable Downs for passengers to watch the gliding, and there were also specials to the Zoo at Whipsnade. The Dance Hall at Dunstable had a bus contract to take its customers home after midnight; five vehicles were normally used.

with a trip to Head Office at Northampton as Chief Traffic Assistant.

At Luton George remembers Barbara Meek and Mrs Cootes, a former Luton Corporation conductress, who was a friend of Barbara and also came into the office. Barbara's husband also worked on the buses. Janet Myers was a typist and Mrs Ethel Newman also worked in the office; her husband was an Inspector, and when he died the cortege passed through the garage at his request. Gillian Brightman also worked in the office, then she married one of the Irish drivers and emigrated with him to Ireland, Janet taking over her post.

George remembers the Friday wages run with amusement. Mr Rumbold, the boss, who nearly always wore sandals, had been allocated a small Austin A30, then a slightly larger A35. He and George were both over 6 feet tall and had a job getting into the car. The Chief Inspector and Driving Instructor came as well, because they were well-built. George would drive and the little car could hardly get up the hill by the bank, with all this muscle on board – this was known as the 'slow get away'! The money was collected before the bank opened at 09.00.

At Luton drivers and conductors seemed to stay together unless there was a conflict of interests.

Luton was always quiet for the factory fortnight and staff could also have holidays then. The engineering staff, on the other hand, worked hard to get up to date with maintenance; the roster was completely redrawn for this time.

The Vauxhall plant used to have three going-home times, 4.30pm, 5.00pm and 5.30pm, and each required 20 vehicles. Some were normal services extended to the works and others were specials.

Eastern National, and later United Counties, was given the option to buy Corporation buses every 10 years or so, and in 1970 this was taken up. No engineers came over, as they were needed for other council vehicle work. Some staff retired or left but the majority of them went to Castle Street when United Counties could not afford to rent the Corporation bus garage. Over a Sunday night all the vehicles moved to Castle Street, which was so crowded that there was a problem getting them out next morning. As most of them were not Bristols – and even the RELLs were manual rather than semi-automatic – they were dispersed throughout the company. This caused a problem with maintenance and drivers 'blacked' them as non-standard. As a result many were sold on and replacement Bristols sought from far and wide.

The former Luton Corporation staff were in a different branch of the union from the United Counties men. As a result, when a strike was called they would sometimes work on without being blacklisted. The union area representatives were also different, so the Corporation men would walk out of any meeting they attended as they would not recognise them as their representatives.

Also causing problems were United Counties crews not wanting former Corporation staff doing runs outside Luton; it was subsequently agreed that this would only happen in emergencies.

At times George had to relieve the Depot Manager at Hitchin, which was about the same size as Aylesbury. In 1974 he became the Area Manager at Bradford, Keighley, Skipton and Ilkley, with West Yorkshire Road Car, and at privatisation in 1979 he transferred to Ribble as an Area Manager.

Following redundancy he and two colleagues from Ribble bought Vale Coaches, until George retired in 1996 and opened a newsagent's shop in Doncaster, where he worked for nine years. He retired again in 2005 and now spends some time at the Sandtoft vehicle preservation site near Doncaster. He also

Inspectors at Luton. Back row, left to right: Tommy Bangs, Bill Smith, Jerry McGrath, Dennis Plater, Dennis Mulligan, John O'Brien and Frank Fortune; middle row: Peter Blessing, Ken Eveleigh, John Hornibrook, Bob Baker, Stan Bryan and Frank Higgins. In the foreground is Alf Shelley, whose retirement was being celebrated. *Angela and John O'Brien collection*

has shares in two former McBraynes coaches, one in Inverness and the other in Edinburgh. He is also the shareholder in a Bristol RELL at the Lincoln Bus Museum. Even though retired he has a part-time job as a driver for Stagecoach (Yorkshire Traction) at Doncaster, his main job being to take children from outlying villages to school in Selby. In late 2008 Stagecoach at Doncaster closed and all buses moved to Rawmarsh Depot.

In later years George's brother went into a new restaurant and was surprised to find that it was owned by former Luton & District Bus Company General Manager Graham Cumming, who had started off as a driver and had become the boss when Luton and Aylesbury were privatised.

Angela O'Brien

Angela had two stints at United Counties. She was a secretary at Luton from 1974 until having her family in 1980, then she returned in 1984 at the request of Dennis Ord, on a temporary contract as Personal Assistant to Bob Rumbold, Area Manager. She has been at both Luton old depot and at the new Arriva depot ever since, and is now the Personnel Assistant to the four Company Directors. Her husband John also worked for United Counties as a driver then an Inspector before leaving to work in the Magistrates

John O'Brien. *NBC News*

Brian Barraclough. *NBC News*

Court at Luton; he now works in London as a Clerk at the Courts.

Angela remembers many of her old colleagues, including Bob Humphreys, who was a Conductor Trainer; Jack King, the Chief Clerk; John Morris, the Depot Superintendent; trainee Roland Higgins; Richard Christian; Janet Fenwick, the other Personal Assistant; Brian Barraclough; and Richard Dyball, as both a conductor and an Inspector. Christine Coates was a clerk who married a driver called Arthur Rose, and still works in Luton for Arriva doing bus stop maintenance. Lewin and Mari Brown were a driver and conductress, Carlo Mastrivall was an Inspector, and Martin Major was another driver. Angela remembers that Mr Rumbold was a keen rabbit farmer and on several occasions came into work with straw on his back.

Angela's main work was answering complaints from passengers and, having arranged meetings, taking and producing the minutes. Another task that she helped with was sorting out the weekly wages if a wages clerk was on holiday or sick. The wages were counted, counted again and checked before being put in the pay packets. It was a nerve-racking job until the last one was done and no money was left.

Brian Barraclough

Brian is a local lad from Luton. He first joined United Counties as a shift fitter at Luton's Castle Street Depot, having being trained in other industries beforehand. He then was promoted to shift chargehand and later Assistant Depot Engineer.

Before privatisation, Brian moved to Milton Keynes City Bus as Area Engineer, where he worked with Steve Appley and Malcolm Parker. The depot at Winterhill was state-of-the-art; Brian's office was at the bus station and the offices at Winterhill were Portakabins in the car park.

Brian then went back to work for the new United Counties as Area Engineer for Bedford, Biggleswade and Huntingdon.

United Counties Engineering had been formed at Bedford Road, Northampton, and was separate from the United Counties depot and Head Office. When Stagecoach Holdings bought the company in 1987 it looked at the site as a potential money-spinner and decided to sell it off and move to a small site in Rothersthorpe Road, Northampton. Bedford became the company's main works, although Northampton was still the Head Office. In 1992 Brian was given the task of closing the Central Works, clearing out the unwanted plant and machinery and moving the rest to Rothersthorpe Road. This was a logistics nightmare but it all worked.

After accomplishing this great feat Brian left Stagecoach and worked for Luton & District at its

Watford Depot as Engineering Manager. When Luton & District subsequently sold out, Brian returned to Luton as Fleet Engineer, the post he has retained since that date for Arriva Shires & Essex.

Graham Cumming

Graham was born in Luton and spent most of his working life based near or in Luton. His first bus job was as a driver for Seamarks Coaches, who specialised in troop movements and tours. His next promotion was as Depot Superintendent at Aylesbury, where he replaced David Shadbolt, who went to Luton. As the boss on £9,800 per annum, Graham was the lowest paid member of staff, as all the others did overtime. The staff complement was 30, and the District Manager at that time was Brian McCall. Graham stayed there until 1983.

The main country service, from Aylesbury, was the 61 route to Luton via Tring and Dunstable. However, a new route to Milton Keynes Central started as the X15 and still runs at the time of writing, although its is less of an express as it calls at most large villages on its route.

In 1985 Graham was Depot Manager at Luton, taking over from David Shadbolt again. This depot was huge by Aylesbury standards and had 15 Inspectors. One day Graham went into their office

Graham Cumming. *Arriva Aylesbury Social Club website*

and found them all asleep; he tactfully walked out and waited for a while, then went back in and found them all hard at work. Nothing was said, but he never found any of them asleep again.

The main checkers-in at Luton were Dennis Mulligan and Peter Blessing, and the Mobile Inspector was Mr Cox. By this time Stan Morris was in charge of the Luton area, and later went on to a job at NBC Headquarters. Andrew Vernon was employed as the company Marketing Manager, based at Luton, and the union men were conductors Danny McGraw and Ted Salmon.

At this time the NBC made the decision to split United Counties into three parts. Luton & District would include Aylesbury, Leighton Buzzard, Luton and Hitchin. The asking price was about £1.9 million; two bids were offered, and the staff bid led by Graham was successful. At the same time Milton Keynes City Bus was sold off, to be run by Jeff Gundell.

John Hargreaves, the man from the NBC, came to talk to Graham, and after they had talked for about an hour John got up from his seat and they swapped chairs. 'This is now your office – get on and run the company,' Graham was told, which was what he did for seven years, until the company was sold at a profit in 1994.

John Brook, Chairman of the NBC, gave Graham and his team a very short time to get going and raise the money. However they achieved this in record time. John Kingham was appointed as Accounting Director at this time, and the Board made three rules for the shareholders.

* If a shareholder was made redundant, or left through illness, they could keep their shares for three years, then they had to sell them back to the company at the going rate.
* Shares could be transferred to a spouse or family on death.
* If a shareholder was sacked, that day's value of the shares was paid out in full.

Graham's first job was to set up the Board of Directors, which included David Abel, Peter Grimes, Ray Garlick, David Cordner, Peter Collins and Chris Pitcher, then to start the job of running the company. Staffing was too high – 14 people were doing the work of nine. Graham worked out a plan to reduce the team by about a third, which was rejected by the Employee Buyout Team as too low. They went away and came back with a lower staff requirement, which was a reduction of 70 staff. No staff would be made redundant if at all possible, and reductions would be by natural wastage. As it happened, more than 70 staff asked to leave, so no one was made redundant. This took about £1 million off the wages bill.

All 700 staff had promised to contribute at least £1,000 towards the cost of buying the company, and most paid it in £10 instalments over a two-year period. Other staff, including Graham, put in all their savings or remortgaged their houses, and the excess was borrowed from the bank. This loan was paid back, with interest, in two years.

The maximum working day was to be 7hr 38min, which was broken down into driving and standby; the 14 separate standby rotas had to go. A group of drivers looked after their own routes with a Team Leader, who sorted out rotas, making sure all duties were covered and all staff had their days off and holidays. Graham had budgeted for each route requiring six buses and 15 drivers; however, this was reduced by three to 12, enabling all drivers to carry on with their overtime as before. This only occurred on some Luton routes, as it was impractical on the others. Previously the staff had worked out a way of calling in sick and enabling their colleagues to work on rest days, with time-and-a-half pay. As passengers began to know their friendly bus drivers they brought their friends and revenue went up 20%.

At the time of sale the company had gone from a share rate of £1 to £7, the turnover had become £86 million and the profit was between £6 and £7 million. This compares with the last year under United Counties, when a £1.3 million loss was recorded.

Graham retired at the age of 59 and now enjoys his life with the family and his hobby of golf.

David Shadbolt

In 1983 David Shadbolt was transferred to Luton from Aylesbury. This was a bit of a culture shock, going from a little family team with a few buses to the largest depot with hundreds of staff, a strong union presence and many challenges to face. At Luton David remembers Bob Rumbold as his Area Superintendent and Brian McCall as Bob's assistant. Another person David remembers was Peter Blessing, who was the Assistant Depot Superintendent.

He remembers that his office in Luton was in the new building above the new maintenance building; the old offices were used by Gordon Dearman as his uniform store.

At the time of reorganisation Luton, Hitchin and Aylesbury were grouped together to be eventually sold off as Luton & District.

Arthur Rose

Arthur arrived from Ireland in 1954 and joined the Royal Fleet Auxiliary branch of the Royal Navy, working out of Portsmouth. In 1960 he moved to Luton and was encouraged to work on the buses. He started as a conductor but rapidly became a driver in 1961. He had two weeks of route learning before his test.

Luton had four types of rotas then: town work, country work, relief coaching and private hire, and full-time coaching work. All drivers started on the town work. Arthur found this boring and successfully applied for country work, which he really enjoyed. In 1962 he applied successfully for the relief coaching and private hire rota, and spent many a happy day travelling to exotic places such as London, Bournemouth, Eastbourne, Clacton, Yarmouth, Ramsgate, Portsmouth and Weymouth, and on private hires to such places as the Wye Valley and the hypermarkets in northern France.

Arthur began an additional career in 1962 when he volunteered to go out to lop trees and service bus stops. To this day he still does this, under contract to Hertfordshire and Buckinghamshire County Councils. This work generated cash for United Counties, and now for Arriva Shires & Essex.

In National Express days Arthur drove from London to Northampton and Nottingham, from Ipswich to Cheltenham (Luton to Cheltenham section), overnights to Stranraer, and to Bradford, Manchester, Colne and Burnley, as well as specials for Celtic Football Club and veteran private hires to the war graves in northern Europe. Arthur's favourite coaches at this time were 168 and 169.

In 1984 United Counties started the privatisation process and Mr Rumbold asked Arthur to do the contract bus stop work as a full-time job. He was given the post of Inspector and had a lad to help him. He used to have responsibility for bus stops in Bedfordshire; the county refused to take over the responsibility and have a contract, which is why Stagecoach and Arriva still look after their own bus stops there.

Christine Coates worked in the office at Castle Street Depot, and she and Arthur married, stayed together until Christine's death a few years ago. In 2002 Arthur officially retired, although he still does relief work as a Controller at Luton and in London. He still does his bus stops in Hertfordshire and is still making money for Arriva; the stops he is now installing are the type that talk to the passengers and can light up.

Dennis Mulligan

Dennis moved to Luton from Ireland in 1959. He started work at the Vauxhall car factory, but did not like being confined in a building for a whole shift, and as a result he left. Thus he arrived at the gates of Castle Street Depot in 1962 and applied to be a bus conductor. He was trained by Joe Donahue and spent three years learning the routes and getting used to the job.

In 1965 Dennis went into the driver training school. He was still learning and was taken out for a test, thinking he was having a lesson. Charlie Smith was the Instructor. Dennis went down Stocking Stone Hill and reversed in Old Bedford Road. Coming back to the depot he was asked a few Highway Code questions by Joe Beckett, then was told that he had passed a test he was not aware he had taken. While reversing he had to open his cab door to see where he was going and to avoid a tree, and the examiner was very impressed by this.

Thus began a driving career that lasted until he retired. Later he was invited by Bob Rumbold to join the coaching team, which was available for relief work on regular services and private hire, as well as being rostered for stage carriage work during the week. The largest amount of private hire work was provided by Vauxhall Motors, which once or twice a year hired 20 vehicles to take staff to places such as Wembley or Oxford. Luton drivers led the way, with vehicles and drivers from other depots helping out. Vauxhall Motors had a very large Sports & Social Club with many facilities. The company employed about 26,000 workers, and at lunchtimes and three times in the evening there were 20 buses available to take them home and fetch the next shift in. Dennis remembers that on the Cutenhoe Estate the bus drove at 10mph and the passengers all got off at their gates instead of at bus stops.

Dennis remembers from his coaching days that Eric Miles was one of the regular drivers on the Portsmouth and Southsea run. Bedford also had a regular driver on this run. They had found a cafe that fed and watered them ready to go back home. One day both of the regulars were away and Dennis was seconded to do the run. Going into the cafe the staff asked him where the regulars were, and Dennis made up a story that one was being married and the other was best man. To the surprise of the regular drivers, the following week they were confronted with a wedding gift. Dennis was given a rocket when they returned, but it was all taken in good spirit.

Later on the coach runs were taken over by the National Express Group, and Dennis and his pal Arthur Rose spent many a happy hour driving all over the country on these services.

Dennis was a union man all his career. He remembers being told that Eric Miles and Les Ogden had started the Luton Branch, and he eventually succeeded Eric as Branch Chairman and spent many hours in the Boardroom at Northampton, negotiating better conditions for his union colleagues.

Dennis remembers one occasion when the buses were cold due to heaters not working. They were 'blacked' by the union and this caused friction with the management. Colin Clubb chaired a regular meeting and requested the reasons for this blacking. Dennis was very forceful in his reply, which took

Colin aback. To Colin's credit he went away and thought about the problem. Ringing up Luton a few days later, he was told that there was still a problem, and he and his driver arrived there later the same day. Colin put on his overalls and got into the pit to help sort out the problem and get the buses back on the road. He earned great respect for doing this.

At the next meeting, at Northampton, Dennis was as quiet as a mouse and Colin asked him why. Dennis replied that Colin knew the problems and had helped to sort them out, and as a result there was not much to say. Colin appeared to appreciate this sentiment and they both went off for lunch feeling satisfied. United Counties at Luton was tolerant of the union and allowed the members to hold meetings in the canteen when required. In the 1970s the union became involved in the 'winter of discontent' and officials found themselves lobbying Parliament in the House of Commons.

Later Peter Blessing arrived at Luton United Counties from the Corporation. Seeing that Dennis was driving, unionising and at that time running the Social Club, he suggested he become an Inspector, to give him more time to do everything. Dennis was opposed to this initially, but thought it through and, after a meeting at Northampton, he applied at the last minute. The 'bush telegraph' had worked and Mr Rumbold was waiting for him on his return. Dennis apologised for not telling Bob what was going on and explained his reasoning. The reply was surprising. 'You have just had your first interview – please arrange with Northampton for your other one, with Ken Eveley.' Within days Dennis was an Inspector. At that time Luton had 12 Inspectors and the Chief Inspector was a Mr Chapman. Dennis remembers that Alf Davy used to work in the office and Brian Horner was the Traffic Manager.

Luton appeared always to have a shortage of staff. Ten new drivers were taken on each week, but unfortunately 15 would leave each week. United Counties managers tried to bring in OMO to help this situation, but Luton gained a reputation for providing an inadequate service as a result. Dennis thought out the problem and at the next Northampton meeting suggested a five-day working week, Monday to Friday, with voluntary working on a Sunday and Saturday as overtime. Dennis was in trouble from the union for suggesting this, and although the management thought it over it was not implemented, but was an example of the union representatives being constructive.

Dennis has been the main force behind the thriving Sports & Social Club at Luton. When he took over the club was in dire straits, but he had turned it around to the point that, when the depot moved to its new site, he was able to open a gym with help from Arriva. The club also has a full-scale championship snooker table, a games room, showers for men and women, and a canteen, which is a privately run venture. All staff were requested to pay a Social Club fee per week, which gave them free access to all facilities.

The Social Club organised trips to the seaside. They do an annual drop-in-session in the afternoon for retired bus people, and retired personnel also get a free meal the year they retire. Other events that Dennis and his team organised included a pantomime for the children and an annual dinner dance, with trips to the horse and dog races. In early years two coachloads used to go to Newport, Gwent, for a weekend out, with visits and clubs to be organised. He has also organised trips to the hypermarkets in northern France.

Dennis also drove private hires for the Magistrates of Luton and area. One day he had the misfortune to loose the organiser, who had decided to wait for late passengers, away from the coach, at Calais. The coach and everyone else got on the ferry but the organiser remained on the quay. Dennis had to organise a passage on the next ferry and waited for the organiser at Dover. Many trips have left passengers behind, but not the organiser!

Donn Goss, Geoff Waters, Norman Mitchell, Dave Priestley, Kath Freeling, Brian Swann, Colin Rutter and Mick Hubbocks, trying to lose weight. *NBC News*

Janet Fennah

Janet Fennah was at Castle Street, then the Arriva garage offices, from 1963 to 2004, with a break in the 1970s and 1980s to spend time with her children. She worked for many of the managers as a Personal Assistant over this period.

She remembers one incident at Castle Street. The reception area was very small, virtually a landing at the top of the stairs. One day a man came for an appointment as a driver. He did not even get into the interview as he unfortunately died while waiting.

Janet remembers Alan Parfitt, George Hawkins and Ray Ramsey from their days at Luton. She was amused to see the photograph of the office and to see her old desk again. She remembers Miss Cherry from Head Office, mainly on the telephone. She also remembers that all office staff had to wear overalls at work.

Colin Rutter

Colin and his friend John White joined United Counties in 1977. Both have worked as drivers for Luton to the present day and both are now approaching retirement. Colin has a scar from Bristol RELL 344 running over his foot by accident one day.

He remembers the Corporation buses well, as he used to live at the end of the 11 Stopsley route. He also recalls that the London Transport Depot was in Park Street and that the buses drove under a house to get into it. When the Leyland Atlanteans arrived they had to go in the back way as they were too long to go through the front entrance.

Colin believes that the best years for buses in Luton were 1988 to 1990 when they were run by Luton & District.

Other Luton memories

Rod Sales remembers one of his weddings well. He and his wife hired the white Luton double-decker bus, which was decked out for them by their colleagues. The parents and the couple had a tour of honour round the town to celebrate. Rod also remembers his stag party well. He and his pals hired a coach and went to London. When the clubs closed, they decided to go boating in one of the parks. Most of them fell in, and Rob lost his clothes at some time during this excursion.

Rod's other claim to fame is that he and a group of colleagues raised more than £1,000 for a local charity by completing many trips round an Army Assault Course. Unfortunately the money was stolen, but the busmen all made sure the correct amount went to the charity out of their own pockets.

One Luton driver mentioned a scam that the coach drivers used to do, which involved two brown envelopes. When collecting tickets, drivers used to put them in an envelope for office use. Some passengers paid the driver and their names and money were added to the envelope. Back at base a second envelope was made out and only the tickets enclosed, leaving the cash for the driver.

Another driver mentioned an incident with an Inspector. The driver was leaving Mansfield and was requested to drop the Inspector before getting onto the M1 motorway; he would then get a lift back to base in the following mini van. However, the driver decided that, as his next scheduled stop was Sheffield Coach Station, he would go by the book and not stop. The result was that the Inspector had a trip to Sheffield and the mini van driver had a day out too.

Mr Mountain used to drive the OMO buses in Luton. The ones he remembers are the 142/145 services to Silsoe and Paxton with the Vauxhall Motors service 13. Mr Mountain also remembers buses 148, 149, 150 and 487. Later he remembers collecting Bristol VRs 852 and 853 from Derby after conversion to power steering. Apparently they wobbled back to Luton, making him feel drunk without drinking.

Another former conductor remembers that he used to enjoy chatting with customers, holding babies for mums sorting out their pushchairs, and the general good feeling between bus crews and passengers. Unfortunately with OMO this disappeared as drivers had less time and more work to do. Some passengers used to give their regular conductors and drivers Christmas presents, which were appreciated for a year's good service.

Another driver remembered that, for the summer factory fortnight, the buses in Castle Street were moved out of the yard and distributed to the local side streets to make way for the hoards of passengers and coaches taking them away for their holidays.

The 1970 United Counties bus strike caused an unfortunate accident. Castle Street had a picket line, and a private coach driver ran over several of the picket members while trying to gain access to the yard with his coach. A court case resulted and compensation was paid.

One year William Price was entered for the Driver of the Year competition, which resulted in his spending a weekend at Blackpool, which he enjoyed. He also did reasonably well for the company.

Both Ray and Ann Garlick worked for the company, and Ray was on the Board of Directors of the privatised Luton & District Bus Company. Others contributing memories were L. Blake, M. Boland, Wendy Butler, May Donahue, P. Leonard and his

The official handover of Luton & District to the new team on 21 August 1987. Those present are Dave Abel, Peter Grimes, Ray Garlick, David Cordner, Graham Cumming, Peter Collins, Peter Manley, Christopher Campbell and Christopher Pitcher.
From 'NBC 1968-1989' by John A. Birks

Rod Sales and Debbie Jacobs on their wedding day. *NBC News*

star pupil Maureen McGovern, John Hughes, Alan King, Peter McEnaney, Mabel Orr, M. Rogers, T. Watersfield, J. Waters and Jimmy Watts. Most felt that their days at Castle Street, during Eastern National, United Counties and Luton & District days, were the happiest and they were one big family. Managers would talk over problems with staff and resolve any issues without formal procedures. Many staff treated Castle Street as their second home, with partners and families welcome under supervision.

Many former staff worked for other companies before coming to Castle Street, notably Luton Corporation Transport, London Transport, Court Line Coaches and the Airport Coach Services. Once in the Castle Street fold many stayed until they retired.

14
Milton Keynes

Milton Keynes Depot at Winterhill was created from Stony Stratford and Bletchley Depots; it was opened in 1983 and closed in 2005.

Graham Cumming

In 1983, after two years at Aylesbury, Graham moved to offices at Milton Keynes Bus Station, where all depots had come together at the state-of-the-art 'biscuit tin' depot. Built to house 300 vehicles, the depot had a fleet of about 50 and the team rattled around in it. At one time the Central Works at Northampton transferred all its painting to Milton Keynes, the staff being bussed there daily.

Union negotiations were a problem at Milton Keynes, as there were two branches, Bletchley and Stony Stratford. The Depot Superintendent was Nick Smith and the Area Manager was a Mr McAllister. This area now covered Aylesbury, Leighton Buzzard and Milton Keynes.

In 1986 Milton Keynes City Bus was formed, and Jeff Gundell had a hard time with the unions when he became Managing Director.

Tom Bates

Tom started work for Milton Keynes City Bus in 1993, so never worked for United Counties or Stagecoach. However, up to 2005 Stagecoach East actually rented space inside the depot at Winterhill. The depot had a large NBC neon sign on the railway side; however, this was never lit as the railway staff complained that train drivers would mistake it for

Top: **The 'upside-down biscuit tin' depot at Milton Keynes. This depot has since been demolished and a DIY store built on the site; the site of the depot is now the store's car park.** *Roger Warwick collection*

Right: **Jeff Gundell.** *Northampton Chronicle & Echo*

a red signal and stop before arriving at the adjacent railway station.

Tom remembers Sammy O'Neil and Graham Wahen, who had known United Counties days. He now works for MK Metro, the successor to MK Citybus. MK Metro was a Julian Peddle creation; Stagecoach bailed him out of a bus business at Caerphilly and the rumour is that it backed him at MK. Stagecoach even painted one of the MK Citybuses in its livery.

Robin Clare

Robin joined the bus industry by learning to drive at London Transport around 1970. His next driving job, from 1978, and his favourite, was working for Oxford/South Midlands at its depot in Wantage. His favourite buses were the AEC Swifts.

For family reasons Robin moved to the new city of Milton Keynes in 1983, which at that time was full of affordable houses. The NBC transfer scheme enabled Robin to get a job with United Counties at its recently opened Winterhill Depot, and he was interviewed at Bletchley for this post. The buses were mainly Bristol VR double-deckers and Leyland National single-deckers, and they rattled around in their vast depot.

The transfer was a bit of a shock for Robin, as Oxford was a former BET company, which was lean and efficient, whereas United Counties was formerly a Tilling company and overstaffed with procedures going back to the Second World War. The term 'ponderous' came to Robin's mind and he noticed that there was a strong revulsion to change among the staff. The Bletchley 'Londoners' and the Stony Stratford 'Cabbages' used to keep themselves separate in the canteen, both feeling that they had little in common with the other.

Planning of services was mainly controlled by Buckinghamshire County Council under Roger Slevin, the enigmatic County Transport Manager. Build an area and feed it with attractive services was the plan. Bus routes originally followed the grid road system, North to South or East to West. Some services had route numbers to show the main

routes used, including the 400 series routes. The 500 series routes were also County Council-controlled. United Counties had little input, but worked with the Councils to provide the vehicles required.

The ideas were new and, to some, exciting. Robin missed the start of the Dial-a-Bus scheme, but other initiatives included the Quad and Junior Quad cards, which were four-journey tickets, while pensioners had ten-journey tickets. The best route in terms of passenger numbers was the Whaddon Way trunk route; two double-deckers were timed 2 minutes apart on this route and both were standing-room-only at the end of the run.

This all came to an end in 1986 with the formation of the Milton Keynes Citybus, and bus deregulation in 1987. Services could now be provided by any registered bus operator. This was a when John Hargreaves, from NBC Head Office, was pushing minibuses for all operators. These had their uses but died out en masse a few years later.

From 1987 to 1990 Robin became a Driving Instructor in Milton Keynes. He went for training to MOTEC, and while he found that he still had an enthusiasm for the driving and instructing job, he was not too enthusiastic about the company. He was also not too happy when his training bus was taken back into the operational fleet and he was given a van in which to teach the drivers. Three to five unskilled people were trained at a time; some lasted up to 6 months, while others lasted for years.

For a few years Robin left Milton Keynes and worked for R&I tours as a Driving Instructor. He then returned to set up an outstation for that company in Milton Keynes. His next job was with an oil company in Saudi Arabia as Operations Manager for the bus transport.

Returning to Milton Keynes, Robin worked for Julian Peddle at MK Metro as driver and scheduler, and has worked for that company ever since. MK Metro is now part of the Arriva Shires & Essex group. The main older staff who are left are mainly the former Stony Stratford ones, including Malcolm Wood, Sid Major and Ricky Main. The Social Club is run by Mike Lay, who is also a long time-server.

15
Rushden

Rushden was a sub-depot of Wellingborough, and at the time of writing still exists, but as a recycling centre.

John Appleton

After getting married in 1967, John transferred to Rushden Depot, which was a very nice depot to work at.

Birch Brothers operated some services south of the town, while others were operated from United Counties Bedford Depot. Bedford services terminated at the railway station, whereas all Rushden-operated services operated from and to the Lightstrung (named after a former bicycle factory adjacent to the bus stop). Birch Brothers had their

'Cabbage' Wiles in one of the Rushden Bristol LDs. *John Appleton collection*

The Lightstrung bus stop on Skinners Hill in Rushden. *Alan Parfitt collection*

A view inside Rushden canteen, with George Spreckley and Mr Clark. *Ann Murdin collection*

own coach station in Higham Road.

The main services were the 413 to Kettering and the 404 service to Northampton via Wellingborough and Earls Barton. Rushden had many saloons (single-deckers) for local village services and the trips to St Neots. The latter services were coordinated to be on Thursday and Saturday market days, and the buses on this service in earlier years were 303 and 306. In later years Bristol LH 400 was used. At one time up to three double-deckers would leave Rushden for St Neots at Bank Holidays, all packed by the time they got there. The crews would have a good break before coming home in the afternoon.

Freddy Price was the Chargehand Cleaner and he cleaned the garage floor regularly with sawdust and diesel oil. The water taps around the depot shone, as did the buses. Freddy used to wash any bus he could get his hands on, sometimes twice a day. One of the cleaners was George Sturgeon. The Engineer was Alan Partridge, whose father Josh had been a driver at Olney.

John remembers that one snowy day bus 932 came to grief at Stanion. It skidded across the road, up the

bank and landed on its side blocking the road. To get it out was a problem, including using adjacent fields. Fortunately only a few windows were broken and the bodywork scratched, and it did not take long to get it back to usable condition.

Albert Brown was a driver who became an Inspector, and one of the conductors was Freddy Hatfield. Joe Robson was another driver and George Spreckley was the Office Clerk.

In 1968 Alfie Lane, known as 'Shady', gave up the job as Driving Instructor at Rushden. The first training bus at Rushden, which John subsequently used as a Driving Instructor, was 438, a Bristol LS. His first trainee was Gordon Panter from Bedford, and both were frightened by the task that day. They persevered and Gordon passed; at the time of writing he is still driving buses in Bedford. John was examined by the company's Driving Examiner, Joe Beckett. In those days John trained drivers from the ranks of the conductors, who had no licences at all. John would be inspected annually, while examining potential drivers, and had to keep up with all the local and national needs of the bus company. The other training problems were associated with services. Some days training buses were used for school runs morning and evening and converted for training purposes in between.

In September 1969 United Counties took over the services, 12 vehicles and staff from Birch Brothers. United Counties operated the services to London,

Driver Albert Brown and conductor Freddy Hatfield enjoy a break on Rushden town service 447 with bus 409. *John Appleton collection*

Welwyn and Hitchin.

Different bus depots used different buses and the staff had to be trained accordingly. For example, the former Birch Brothers coaches were Leyland Leopards, which were freezing. However, they were fast, but their speed was not matched by their braking power. The 170 series were the better ones of the three types; others were in the 180 and 190 series. The 190s were the worst and the draughts were a severe problem; their windscreens would sometimes freeze on the inside as well as the outside.

One day 192 hit a cow while being driven by Eric Auty, on Hammer Hill near Cotton End. The head of the cow went through the front of the bus and finished up on the steps inside. 192 was repaired and rebuilt with a Seddon front, new entrance doors and steps. Eric reckoned that the cow was doing about 70mph at the time of the impact!

To make the London service more attractive, United Counties took delivery of Bristol RE dual-purpose vehicles, and three were allocated to Rushden. John felt that these were splendid vehicles and very attractive in their all-over cream livery with green waistband. They were numbered 278, 279 and 281.

United Counties took on many former London Transport drivers, who came up with the London Overspill to local towns. These had to be retrained to the Bristol bus, as they were used to different engines and gearboxes.

John Childs, Bob Rumbold and Doug Elphee with Chief Police Inspector R. Green at John Appleton's Safe Driving Award ceremony. *NBC News*

Roger Smith

Roger worked for Birch Brothers at Rushden and transferred to UCOC in 1969 with DUC 70-73C, 82/83 CYV and 90-95 FXD, all Leyland Leopards.

Roger Smith and his wife. *Mick Hedge collection*

Rushden Bristol FS 713 at Kettering with its crew. *Photobus*

He remembers the other drivers and conductors he worked with, such as Albert and Chris Brown and Arthur Hunt. Roger worked on the union committee with Fred Parker, John Mumford and Albert Brown. He also remembers Superintendent Len Gentle, known locally as 'Harry Worth', and Inspector Peter Dickens.

At Rushden there were OMO drivers, crew drivers (working with a conductor) and conductors. Roger still has his jacket, badge and licence badge (EE47831); if you lost this you had to pay 2s 6d for a new one. Some drivers only had single-decker driving licences and could not drive double-deckers, whereas if you had a double-decker licence you could drive both. Drivers had a paper licence as well as the badge.

Roger remembers that Bristol FLFs 635/636 BRP were mainly used on the 413 to Kettering, the Irthlingborough Laundry school runs and the 403/404 runs to Northampton. Other buses were the other Rushden RELHs 213, 279, 281, 287 and 293, and the three Bristol FSs, KBD 713-715D; KBD 713 had a quick clutch stop and was the best one. Another vehicle Roger remembers was Bristol RELL RBD 327G, which used to work the service to London (203), although it had a propensity to set fire to itself. Sometimes this service needed a duplicate and Bristol VR XBD 769J would be used.

While on Friday and Saturday standby turns, the evening crews used to frequent the Wheatsheaf pub in Rushden. Some turns were known by the number of pints that could be drunk at various pubs; one was even known as a seven-pint turn.

When the Birch Brothers buses were taken over the garage parking area was too small, so a piece of land at Skinners Hill was used to park buses. This was also useful when the garage was updated.

In 1978 Roger moved to Shelton Osborn Coaches, then four years later came back to UCOC, working with Bristol RELH dual-purpose coach WBD 290H at Thrapston. There were two shifts at Thrapston, so Roger became friendly with all his passengers, and when an Inspector got on at Woodford, telling Roger off (tongue in cheek), his passengers defended him. Another Inspector told Roger off for not carrying his faretables on the bus; they were still on the kitchen table as Roger could remember every fare. He still has the last faretables he was issued.

Roger had a shock one day when the roving Inspector at Woodford was Arthur Ford from Bedford, deputising for the usual two Inspectors who covered Wellingborough, Kettering and Corby.

Occasionally Roger used to cover coach turns and remembers the 297 service to Milton Keynes and the 378 to Aberdeen. Other services he recalls were the 422 and 423 OMO services to Irthlingborough. One day he arrived at Woodford with Bristol LS KNV 32 to be greeted by Inspector Eddie Powley complaining about the late arrival of the bus.

In more recent years Roger has been a coach driver again and is active in the preservation field, remembering especially trips to the Blackpool bus rally. Roger was also the regular driver of United Counties' most famous Bristol VR, GRP 794L. With Steve Loveridge he was instrumental in its long life with United Counties and its eventual preservation.

The last trip from Rushden to Amsterdam, organised by Tony Kenyon, Brian Mills, Peter Dickens, Ernie Michel and Derrick Warboys (third from left). *NBC News, Steve Loveridge collection*

When Rushden Depot closed in 1978 conductor David Farrar was so affected that he wrote this note of condolence.

FARRAR. D.R. BOX 412.
THIS IS THE LAST ONE THEY'LL
BE NO MORE.
WHO KNOWS WHAT THE FUTURE
HAS GOT IN STORE,
I'VE BEEN A CONDUCTOR FOR
OVER EIGHT YEARS.
BUT AS I GO FROM THE DEPOT
MY EYES FILL WITH TEARS
THE END.

16
Stamford

Stamford was the most northerly of the United Counties depots, and was a sub-depot of Kettering.

Howard Butler

Howard's grandparents lived in Stamford and from a young age he used to go there on visits. The original bus depot was at the wharf, where a builder allowed the vehicles to be parked on his premises. In later years a small depot was opened in the railway station yard.

The original bus station was in Station Road and was a series of bus stands. Later a bus and coach station was built in the square by the sheep market. United Counties buses had one island, Eastern Counties a second, Lincolnshire a third and other local operators used the others. The coaches had their own parking area. Friday was the busiest day as it was market day, when the square was normally full with up to 25 vehicles.

Long-distance coaches used to use Stamford as their toilet, coffee and lunch stops. Originally the A1 road went straight through the centre of the town, although it has since been bypassed. Stamford was always a bottleneck, as the main crossroads were controlled by a policeman and there was a very narrow street. Up to 12 United Auto Services Coaches used to be frequent customers, as well as Eastern Scottish and Western SMT. Morning breaks were between 10.00am and 12 noon, while the evening breaks were between 9.00pm and 10.00pm.

Mick Draper

One turn at Stamford was called 'the lump', which was a long turn and involved Stamford to Oakham, then to Uppingham and finally back to Stamford. For

Stamford Depot was built in National Bus Company days. *Roger Warwick collection*

A driver and conductor rest at Stamford before going to Corby on the 274. *Howard Butler*

Stamford Bus Station with coaches on their breaks. *Howard Butler*

A driver at Stamford Bus Station. *Alan Parfitt collection*

Driver Jack Storey.
NBC News

customers on this service an unofficial 'get you home with your shopping' service was provided – hence 'the lump', as the driver had to lump bags on and off the bus.

The Stamford inspector was Fred Tongue. One day he met a driver and checked his waybill. There was nothing on it and the driver said he would make it up at the end of the day. This was a surprise to Fred, but was a common occurrence then.

Mick remembers that a Stamford driver, Jack Storey, had a job for life. This was due to United Counties taking over his family business

and his lifetime's work was a condition of the sale. Jack retired in 1975 with just under 50 years of service under his belt. He had worked with his father in the Stamford Bus Company, which had six buses and was taken over by United Counties in 1934. Jack was a driver and conductor with United Counties. Stamford had double-deckers until 1970, and he drove to Northampton on some workings. After 1970 Stamford had a fleet of single-deckers and the furthest they travelled was Corby.

Gerald Mead remembers that Stamford only had three buses and ten staff.

17
Stony Stratford

Stony Stratford was a sub-depot of Northampton. In the 1980s it was combined with Bletchley to form Milton Keynes Depot.

Roger Warwick was the Depot Superintendent from June 1973 until the summer of 1975. Tony Townsend was on the engineering side and a great colleague. One day he decided to change jobs as he could not afford to live on his wage, and his whole team decided to do the same.

Brian Allen was a driver and John Rogers assisted Tony. On the union side were Charlie Thorne, Gray and Sid Major. Bonnie Temple was also there, and

Tommy Mathews was a very dependable driver. Albert Caple, Mr Brown, Mr Humberstone and Mr Saville were all old hands, and Mrs Saville was a cleaner. The Inspector was Jack Wilkinson.

Tony and Della Townsend

The Townsends moved to Stony Stratford in 1966 when Tony became the new Foreman at the garage. He was surprised to find that the fitters only greased up buses and changed minor parts; they were mainly unskilled, one having started out as a jockey. All other work had to go to Northampton Depot. The toolbox was empty and they only had one pit to work in. The fleet comprised about 25 vehicles in the early 1970s, and there was a sub-depot at Tavistock Street, Bletchley, where the fitters from Stony would go and work on the buses as and when required.

Other staff at Stony Stratford included Keith Parsons, Jack and Peggy Wilkinson in the office, Inspector Lambert at Bletchley, and cleaner Vi Saville.

The social life at Stony Stratford was quite good, and one event included them all 'going native', as can be seen in the accompanying photograph.

Tony was having a job making ends meet. Engineers were on low pay compared with their colleagues, so he decided to get a job outside the company and was accepted. He informed the new Depot Superintendent, Roger Warwick, who was incensed by the situation. As a result the Chief Engineer rang Tony and upped his pay at once.

The traffic and engineering teams got on well at Stony Stratford. One day Tony took Roger Warwick out to a breakdown to see what was involved. Roger and Tony had known each other for ages, as Roger was a bus spotter when Tony was at Northampton.

One day Victor Bush and Tony got their photos in the local paper for

Stony Stratford Depot. *Roger Warwick collection*

Stony Stratford Safe Drivers, S. Carr, B. Allen and Albert Caple, with Teddy Dravers in 1974. *NBC News*

A December 1975 dinner at Stony Stratford, with Norman and Mrs Maycock, and Norman and Mrs Reader next to Judith and Colin Clubb. *Colin Clubb collection*

being 'Knights of the Road'. Victor took a lady home to Northampton when the last bus broke down, while Tony organised a relief vehicle when a driver failed to go to work and arranged an onward connection to Newport Pagnell.

When the Townsends moved to Stony Stratford, Tony's wife Della retired as a conductress, but later helped to clean the buses. One of the most hated jobs was to clean the inside ceilings. In the 1960s and 1970s smoking was still allowed on buses and the cream ceilings were stained brown, but with elbow grease, soap and water it was cleaned off.

Albert Caple with Red Indian brave Tony Townsend, his squaw Della Townsend and little braves. *Tony and Della Townsend collection*

While Tony was at Stony Stratford a new door was put in the back of the depot building, and the back yard was used for this photograph to mark Fred Richards's retirement. On the back row (left to right) are Vic Bush, Ray Grant, Sid Abbott (with cap, Tony's predecessor), Peter Valentine, a young apprentice, Mick Russell and John Rogers. On the front row are Johnny Johnson, Fred and Mrs Richards, Vi Saville and Tony Townsend. *Tony and Della Townsend collection*

Tony remembers that one of the old Bristol L Type single-deckers had been sold to Abbey CofE School in Bletchley, who called her 'Abigail'. She used to appear at Stony Stratford annually for her inspection and MOT exam. *NBC News*

Another old London bus dropped in one day and slept overnight at Stony Stratford, Tony Townsend and his apprentice putting it to bed. *Tony and Della Townsend collection*

However, the brown dirty water would run down Della's arms and she would need a good clean when she was finished – an early way of getting a fake tan!

The other jobs Della did for United Counties were mainly non-paid. When Tony moved to Kettering, a fleet of new minibuses had to come down from Scotland, and Della was one of the team that went up to collect them. In earlier years she had been courted in a United Counties lorry, had travelled to and from home in a United Counties van, and had travelled to Lowestoft for days out collecting Lodekkas from Eastern Coach Works.

A banquet dinner at Combe Abbey, Coventry, including Colin Stafford on the right. *Tony and Della Townsend collection*

Della and Tony with Johnny and Mrs Johnson (centre) at another dinner. *Tony and Della Townsend collection*

18
Thrapston

Thrapston was a sub-depot of Kettering.

Mick Cornwell

Mick works out of the Thrapston outstation at present, and remembers colleagues Ernie Headland (driver), Walt Wilson (conductor), Roy Turner (driver), Bill White (who went to work at Kettering), Bob James, Bob Jones and Agi Moor (a conductress at Rushden). Mick has lived at Thrapston all his life and is a well-known driver in the local area. He must have impressed one of his passengers so much that Kim Chambers is also now a driver at Thrapston outstation.

Mick started with United Counties in 1968, and his brother Peter was also employed as a conductor. In the early days Thrapston had two OMO turns and two crew turns. Bob Jones was permanently on the OMO turn and the other was covered by Mick and Roy, week on, week off; they crewed on the other week.

Thrapston gradually became three OMO turns, but was then closed down for five years. Mick transferred to Kettering until Thrapston was reopened by Stagecoach. The outstation then had Mick, Roger Smith (who became an Inspector) and Barry Hinde (who later went into the office at Kettering), and their regular buses were 794 (Roger) and 811 (Mick), while Barry drove both. Their other Thrapston colleagues have included Keith Gwynne, Glen Harvey, Rod Clark, Steve Fisher and Ted Melia.

Mick works at Kettering in the summer holidays and does driving when required, returning to Thrapston for school work in September. In recent years the main job has been the Thrapston to Raunds bus and the market day Thrapston to Northampton bus. Mick has a friendly outlook on life and enjoys meeting his old and young customers.

Over the years the buses at Thrapston have stayed in various sheds and yards, including Thrapston Council yard, the cattle market, a garage in Huntingdon Road and next to Hammonds Turkeys, which is now Tilleys Sweets; both the latter places had some weird smells as Mick passed by! In one of the garages the buses were plugged into the electricity to keep the engines warm overnight, enabling them to start easily in the morning. In later years the roof came off when a taller bus tried to go into the shed. When parked at the cattle market, some buses went for drives overnight as a local lad decided to take them out for a spin; the market was not used after that.

Mick is now known by the second and third generations of some families and is more of a friend than someone who drives a bus. He is flexible with dropping off his passengers if they have heavy shopping or are older or disabled.

He started off with single-decker half-cabs, while in later years the buses have been double-deckers, the first being Bristol VRs and later Leyland Olympians. Trees have not presented too much of a problem around Thrapston, as the tree-lopper used to call regularly. Since this was discontinued, the local council has performed the same function. Some of the lanes are very narrow and with extra bush growth the bus has to push its way through. Fortunately, farmers do cut the hedges occasionally.

19
Toddington

Toddington outstation. *Roger Warwick collection*

Toddington was an outstation of Luton, and Alan Parfitt remembers that the depot usually held two double-deckers. Numbers 527, 564, 603 and 608 were stationed there, 603 being in poor condition.

George Hawkins adds that Toddington had two buses with five crews. Two 7ft 6in buses would fit into the depot, but it was too narrow for two 8-foot buses. In the latter case one bus stayed in the street. The main services, to Toddington, were the 54 from Ampthill to Luton and the Luton Corporation service 3 from Toddington to Luton. Most of the 54s only worked to Toddington. Bedford to Whipsnade Zoo services also called at Toddington.

20 Welford

Welford was an out-station of Northampton.

William Bazeley

Sheila Nunn contributes these memories of William Bazeley, who was a driver at Welford, starting in 1936 and finishing in 1969. The family moved to Welford in 1937; until then William cycled to work each day from Northampton. Other staff recalled are drivers Jim Davis and Mr Eames, and conductors Len Oxley, Len Savage and Len Bell.

Summers were hot in Welford and winters were cold; buses were equipped with spades and chains in the winter. The main services operated were from Welford to Market Harborough and Northampton, with three buses. The bus garage was at the bottom of West Street, near the Swan Inn.

The drivers and conductors were very dedicated and did their

Welford Depot. *Roger Warwick collection*

William and Mrs Bazeley. *Sheila Nunn collection*

William Bazeley is in the background of this photograph with a colleague in the Welford snow of 1947. Grandpa Bazeley is in the foreground. *Sheila Nunn collection*

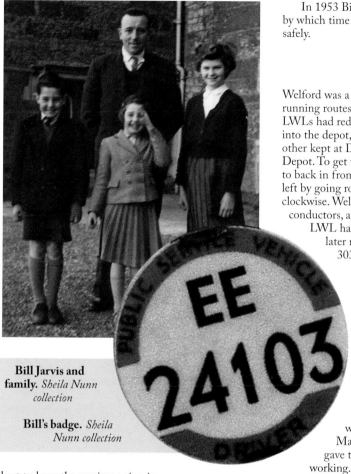

Bill Jarvis and family. *Sheila Nunn collection*

Bill's badge. *Sheila Nunn collection*

In 1953 Bill received a certificate for safe driving, by which time he had driven some 250,000 miles safely.

Fred Moore

Welford was a self-contained unit, with three vehicles running routes 312, 316, 317 and 320. The Bristol LWLs had reduced-height destination boxes to get into the depot, which held two vehicles with the other kept at Derngate Bus Station or Northampton Depot. To get two vehicles into the shed one had to back in from the right and the other from the left by going round the village clockwise or anti-clockwise. Welford's staff included five drivers and five conductors, and the buses included 35-seater Bristol LWL half-cabs 345, 346 and 355, which were later replaced by Bristol SUL4As 301, 302, 303.

Market Harborough Bus Station held 30 vehicles, and on Tuesday market days it was full. Other operators using the bus station were Midland Red from Coventry and Leicester, N&S Coaches, and Central Coaches from Uppingham. Route 259 needed relief vehicles on market days.

Fred remembers that Welford had a hand water pump. The toilets were at the Swan pub, round the corner, which was also the company agent.

Many pubs were company agents, which gave the crews an excuse for a sly drink while working.

Hopefully one of the Welford buses would start in the morning, collect all the village passengers and return to the depot. If the second bus would not start, the passengers pushed it down the slight hill to bump-start it.

Life at the outstations was completely different from the main depots. Everyone, including passengers, mucked in with all the jobs. Occasionally the crews were given gifts, including cigarettes at Theddingworth and wood at Marston Trussell. One day the 316 service loaded the boot with wood and went to Northampton. On arrival the Inspector swapped the bus so that it could go to Bedford Road for a service and repaint. Three weeks later it arrived back, complete with the wood.

At one pub the crew were invited in for a drink while waiting for the pub's landlady to get ready to go to town. The Inspector arrived and the crew were tipped off that he was coming. The landlord put them in the kitchen where there were the remains of breakfast on the table. When the Inspector arrived they were finishing off their breakfast while the landlord got them out of trouble.

best to keep the services going in all weathers. Their work started very early to clear the bus garage entrance of snow, allowing the buses out. William was awarded safe driving awards during his 30 years service.

Uniforms were a white smock in the summer and a grey uniform in the winter.

Bill Jarvis

Sheila Nunn also tells us of Bill Jarvis, who also worked at Welford and was William Bazeley's brother-in-law. He worked for the company from 1949 to 1955, driving single- and double-decker buses.

One day Bill was driving a bus on black ice, and it did a complete circle in the road before continuing. When the road was measured it was only 6 inches wider than the length of the bus.

On the last journey at night the money was counted on the back of the bus. Coins and notes were put on the flat seat, and if the driver braked hard the money would scatter all over.

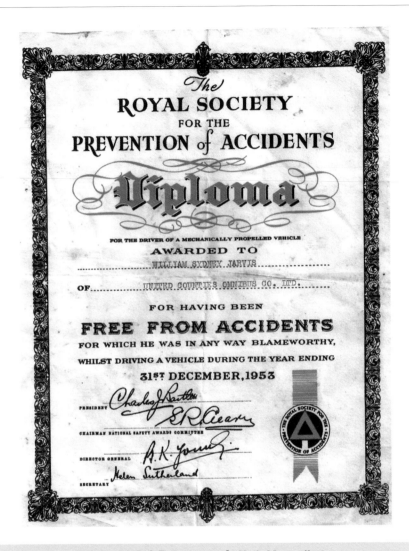

Bill Jarvis's Safe Driving award. *Sheila Nunn collection*

Each conductor used to have a book of parcels tickets, which were filled in by hand and stuck to the parcel.

Norman Maycock at Derngate Bus Station could not understand what happened at the outstations and why they were not run the same as Derngate.

When the schedules were changed, the Welford men would not do them unless they agreed that they were suitable. All conductor training at Welford was done by the other conductors, while the drivers went to Northampton.

Opposite: **Wellingborough St Johns St Bus Garage in 1942. In the front row are driver Josh Partridge (left), third from left is cleaner Ms Bullock, and next Alan Partridge. The second row includes cook Mrs Moore and conductress Mrs Jowell; the fifth lady was conductress Mrs Moore, then Bel Coles and conductress Doreen Cleavley/Knighton sitting on her driver's knee. Bel Coles was the only lady driver at Wellingborough at that time. In the next row are Inspector Bert Kenyon, drivers Mr Boswell and Mr Mabbutt, driver George Neal (fifth from left), driver Mr Sturgess (fifth from right), driver Stan Parker, Ralph Golding, Inspector Geoff Manning, and Flo and Ben Ascombe. The back row includes, from the left, drivers Stan Vorber and Mr Sturgess, Jock Cockings, and storeman Bob Woods.** *Doreen Cleavley collection*

21
Wellingborough

Wellingborough was a main depot with Rushden as a sub-depot.

Wellingborough Depot. *Roger Warwick collection*

Doreen Knighton (née Cleavley)

Doreen was a Wellingborough girl and went to work in the local industry of boots and shoes. In 1941 she was conscripted to work for the nation and opted for a job as a conductress on the buses. She worked on the buses until 1946 and still meets up with people she met in those days. One of those is Eileen Roberts, who was also a conductress. After her stint, Doreen went back to finish her career in the boot and shoe industry.

Mr Dickerson

Mr Dickerson's son tells us that his father worked for Wellingborough Omnibus Company and United Counties for 40 years. He lived in Irthlingborough and died in 1971. They remembered Aunt Florrie's

Teashop and the bus garage nearby for one single-decker, which used to work to Woodford. His father was involved in the strike at Irthlingborough, which was very violent, when passengers refused to use buses. He occasionally worked the Cheltenham coaches.

The 10.00pm bus to Chelveston, from Rushden, was known locally as the 'Drome' bus as it terminated at the Chelveston Air Base. One day the driver took a girl with him on his lap to the 'Drome'.

Father was teetotal, but other drivers used to drink while laying over at Raunds and in the Wheatsheaf pub in Rushden. During the war he was in the Home Guard at Rushden Depot and remembered that they had guns but no bullets. He worked on the late-night buses at Kettering and remembered the 'Swinger' services from the cinemas to local estates and villages.

Now all Northampton buses go down his road at half-hour intervals and it takes 1¼ hours to get to Northampton rather than the 1 hour it used to take. The quickest way to Northampton used to be by train to Wellingborough and then on to Northampton, which, he remembers, took about three-quarters of an hour. Today Mr Dickerson uses his free pass to travel locally and pays £1 to go to Northampton, Bedford and Milton Keynes, services that he finds useful.

Ann Murdin

Ann worked at Wellingborough as a cashier until the depot closed in 1986. She then transferred to Kettering and has now worked for the company for more than 40 years. She remembers Kathleen McGowan, the two Probate sisters (one of whom was called Ruby) and Maisie Bailey.

Ann vividly remembers her 21st birthday. She was manhandled onto the roof of a double-decker, which was driven into the middle of the depot and left there. Eventually she was rescued by the Depot Manager, who arranged for the bus to be brought back to the stairwell.

Ann remembers Mick Dunn, who used to film and take photographs of all events at Wellingborough; he made a video film of the Wellingborough closure and reunions.

Ann also remembers the Corby steelworks buses and the stops made at Burton Lane chip shop on the way home. She had a problem the first time she took a Leyland National to Rushden. The bus shelters at Skinners Hill were right by the road and she accidentally clipped one as she left the stop; the Nationals had a longer back end than other vehicles.

United Counties' first Leyland National is seen at the Ise Lodge Estate in Kettering with Chris Downes at the wheel. *Kettering Evening Telegraph*

Once, while a conductress, she rushed down the stairs of the bus and carried on through the open back and into Saxby's pie shop in Midland Road, Wellingborough. The customers were amazed!

Ann mainly drives in Wellingborough on the relatively new Wellingborough Connect services W1 and W2. All her customers are regulars and at Christmas she has many presents and cards from them. She provides a social service as well as a bus service.

Bev Watson

Bev was educated at Wellingborough Grammar School and joined Wellingborough Depot as a conductor in 1973. He followed his father on to the buses, and remembers going out with his father and hiding under the stairs. He is a now a driver at Chowns Mill outstation, near Irthlingborough. He is also an enthusiast who part-owns a former United Counties Bristol FS 651 at Rushden Historical Transport Society.

Bev's impression was that Wellingborough Depot staff liked to do everything differently from other United Counties depots. If all the others did a job one way, Wellingborough would do it another.

Ron Garon, complete with pipe, taught him to drive. His favourite non-Bristol buses were Leyland Nationals 521 and 571, as they were the fastest.

Bev Watson at Wellingborough Grammar School. *Author's collection*

Des arrives back at Greyfriars Bus Station, Northampton, after his last run. *Des Banyard collection*

Des receives his 25-year award from Lord Bill Morris. *Des Banyard collection*

Des Banyard

Des started his career at Wellingborough as a conductor for United Counties and finished it as a driver with Stagecoach at Northampton, on a workers' special, with Leyland/ECW Olympian ARP 608X. For much of his career he also was working for the TGWU as a local representative. He proudly owns a trophy for 25 years' service

with the union, which was presented to
him by Lord Bill Morris, at that time
the General Secretary of the Union.
Des's outside contact with the union,
Mr Buckingham, was not allowed on
United Counties premises, so their
meetings were held outside in the street.
The first strike at Wellingborough had
been in 1936.

Des was instrumental in negotiating
the one-man-operated (OMO)
agreement with United Counties at
Wellingborough, an agreement that
was adopted by other depots soon
afterwards.

With his friend Ron Garon, Des
remembers that staff used to walk
or cycle to work in the early years,
including some from Earls Barton,
Mears Ashby, Irthlingborough and
Finedon. There were two types of rotas:
32 hours a week, which was guaranteed,
and 48 hours a week, which was not.
There was an extra payment of 11d per
hour paid for this rota.

Forty-three duties were covered at
Wellingborough, plus two part-time
duties. Duties were fixed for ages in
those days. Each one was pasted on a
wooden board and a daily waybill was
kept with it, to record passenger numbers and the
amount taken.

In the early days Willibrew tickets were issued,

Bill and Helen Grundy. *Mick Hedge collection*

**The Enquiries office at Wellingborough, which eventually
became the Depot Manager's Office.** *Roger Warwick collection*

then in later days the Setright machines became
common. Later still were the automated machines
such as Wayfarers. The former issued orange tickets
for singles and white for returns; they had a guillotine

to cut out the day, time and date of purchase, and the cut-outs were collected at the depot for counting.

At Wellingborough Des remembers that the toilets and canteen were upstairs while the crew rooms and offices were downstairs. In later years the booking office, then the lost property office, became the Depot Manager's Office.

There were two pits in the back right-hand corner of the depot. The body man was Stan Palmer and the fitter in charge was Fred Austin. In the office was Fred Langley, and Val Everard was the cashier. The building behind the garage was used as a tyre store; this had originally been built as a servicing bay for the gas-powered vehicles used during the war.

Des was personally upset when Wellingborough Depot closed in 1986 with little warning. However, he and some of his colleagues transferred to Northampton. Kettering and Bedford were also strengthened by the addition of several Wellingborough staff. This was about the same time as the crewed vehicles finished on United Counties services.

Some colleagues he remembers are George Packwood, Bill Grundy, Albert Loveday, Charlie Haines, Eddie Brown and Charlie King. As his driver,

Des remembers mentioning to Eddie Brown that he should not let students ring the bell and open and close the doors while he was taking the fares; this was prohibited by the PSV code and the Company Rules.

Ron Garon

Ron's bus memories go back to his childhood. His father worked and lived in Irthlingborough and also at Wellingborough when he first started in 1919. He walked to the depot each morning and would sometimes be sent home as there was no work to do. Eventually he was taken on and worked there for many years, driving A to C Type Leyland double-deckers. When they moved to Wellingborough the company gave Mr Garon Snr a moving allowance to buy a bungalow.

Ron became a conductor in 1935 then a driver, and in later years was one of the driving instructors. He was given two awards, for 25 and 40 years with United Counties, and left in 1980 after 45 years.

The bus depot at Wellingborough was built on what was known as Barkers Yard; the land behind it was a fairground. The bus services that Ron enjoyed were the workers' services; he remembers particularly

Wellingborough pits and the Foreman's office. *Roger Warwick collection*

The 'Rapidway' bus in Wellingborough. The passengers are all United Counties staff, including Steve Loveridge, Colin Gayton and Tony Kenyon. 'Rapidway' was designed by Mr McRoberts, the Depot Superintendent. *From 'NBC 1968-1989' by John A. Birks*

the services from Ideal Clothiers to Wollaston (2) and Earls Barton (1). Buses used to go up Cannon Street in those days and it was quite tight if they met another vehicle coming down.

Ron can just remember buses with open staircases at the rear; 191 was the last he saw, and 624 was a former London Transport AEC vehicle. Apparently the brakes were not very good and the driver had to be very careful approaching junctions. Ron recalls that the Bristol FLF buses were very difficult to steer due to not having power steering and because of their size compared with KSWs and other Lodekkas. He remembers having to stand up to drive some buses round corners. The Tilling Group originally used Leyland engines, but in later years they transferred to Gardners, which Ron preferred.

During the war, lights in buses were covered and it was very dark to see your way around.

Ron remembers that some conductors tried to fiddle the company by using tickets more than once and taking the profit, but once found out they were dismissed. Another fiddle was to cash up early, do a

Ron Garon (right) receives one of his long-service awards from Derek Fytche. *Ron Garon collection*

Ron (third from right, back row) with others including John Tate, Barbara Eyles, Lucy Kidder, Peter Clack, Martin Kelly, Mal Cox, Tom White, Tony Townsend, Mrs Abele, Dennis Noon, Rance Muskett, Tom Smith, John Smith, Norman Redhead, Derek Fytche and Jeannie Warwick at an award ceremony. *Ron Garon collection*

last run and keep the money.

Seniority at Wellingborough was by years served, and senior drivers had the pick of the turns.

Ron's favourite training bus was OBD 903. When he was a coach driver he remembers that a day's routing would be Wellingborough to Coventry empty, full from Coventry to Cheltenham, then full back to Wellingborough. He remembers colleagues such as Mal Cox, who was a driver and Inspector, and driver Ron Faulkner. Poor Ron used to have tricks played on him by Ron Faulkner, who wound his seat right down so he would not be able to see out of the window. Ron used to like the turns to Harrold and Odell, as he had relations there and would pay them a visit. Some drivers and conductors would stop in Finedon and hot meals would be sent to Wellingborough for staff by their families.

Buses used to be repaired as they went along.

One incident involved Mr Jewitt, Bill Hayes and a screwdriver to start a bus. On another occasion Bill Hayes's son was underneath the bus watching the flywheel going round as the bus went along.

Kevin Saunders

Kevin worked at Wellingborough from 1976 until it closed in 1986, then he transferred to Milton Keynes. However, he did not like that and in 1994 transferred to Kettering. He started as a conductor, crew driver, OMO driver, then driver. Ron Garon, who always smoked a pipe, taught him to drive. He recalls that Tony Kenyon was the Depot Engineer at Wellingborough, but that he left and went to work for Crosville at Rhyl. He also remembers Roy Wesley, Mick Perry and Peter Knapton.

Kevin was a member of the Wellingborough skittles team. Many former Wellingborough men are members of the Buffs Association.

Mick Dunn

Mick joined United Counties in 1973 at Wellingborough as a conductor, and recalls that the breakdown truck was an ex-Army vehicle with a gun turret. He still works for United Counties' successor Stagecoach East, driving at Northampton.

Mick Hedge

Mick Hedge started his career as a tree surgeon in the Royal Parks in London. He then moved to Wellingborough and worked for the local council, spending the winter trimming trees and the summer cutting grass. He then decided to try something different, and joined United Counties in 1977 after talking to Mrs Helen Grundy in the office and filling in a form. He became a conductor, which involved two weeks' training at Northampton, then in 1979 the Chief Examiner, Norman Redhead, passed him out as a driver. Mick remained at Wellingborough until it closed in 1986. One day in the 1970s he remembers that the snow was so dense and high that four buses were marooned at Raunds, and Mears Ashby was unreachable, marooned by snowdrifts.

Mick remembers that the fitters were Derrick Warboys, Dave King, Steven Palmer and Colin Palmer, Mrs Mary Hedge was the secretary, and Tony O'Leary also worked in the office. The cleaners included Messrs Dodson, Perry and Semnall. Ron Evans was the tyre fitter, working for Michelin tyre company; he moved to Kettering when Wellingborough closed, and at the time of writing still works there. The back shed was mainly the tyre store, but it also housed the dart board and the pool and skittles tables. There was a large area of rough ground at the rear of the depot, which United Counties used to park withdrawn vehicles. Many items from these vehicles were taken for personal preservation by Wellingborough staff.

Three of his fellow drivers, Tony Winch, Vince Cleary and Graham Truett, originally worked at

Peter Knapton and Ernie Barrett. *Mick Hedge collection*

Photographer Mick Dunn with Jean Saunders. *Mick Hedge collection*

Rushden. Mick Mobbs at Kettering had a father who drove at Rushden. Other drivers remembered, some of whom are still driving, are Ian Howie, Kevin Baxter, Dick Gayton, Dave Anderson, Glen Stewart, Trevor Edwards and Steve Goulden. Albert Brown was one of the Inspectors, having been a driver at Rushden. One driver was too tired to cycle to work on some days and would be given a lift by a passing bus, his cycle boarding the bus through the emergency door.

Conductors included Eddie Brown, Len Rowell (who taught Mick to conduct), Ernie Michel, Charlie

Patel, Ron Haynes and Ben Desai. The conductors' room was next to the office, on the ground floor, and contained the lockers, notice board and cashing machines. All money was bagged into bank bags and placed in a canvas bag with the waybill. The lockers had a rear door by means of which the office staff could check the machine details. Mick used to get some overtime as other older conductors would swap a late turn to get home to the family.

Len Rowell did not like issuing the Weekly Tickets as needed, but instead used to write them out beforehand. This rebounded on him one day as he had done them and turned up to find he was on strike; he then had to explain himself to the Inspector.

Eddie Brown was a very outgoing conductor. He used to play Father Christmas, and helped young ladies off the bus with their pushchairs and children. One day he was so engrossed in this occupation that he did not notice that a passenger had rung the bus bell and the bus had left him behind.

Mick Dunn and Mick White arrive at the garage having completed a run on the 401 service from Northampton. The bus is EBD 682C. *Mick Dunn collection*

Mick Hedge and Charlie Patel prepare for their next duty with the now preserved 651 EBD outside Wellingborough Depot. Above the bus is the canteen window. *Kevin Lane collection*

Wellingborough snowplough 467 in operation. *John Appleton collection*

Soldiers were issued with an MOD pass, which was exchanged for a ticket and put in with the waybill. Northamptonshire Social Services also issued passes for some of its clients visiting prisoners.

The canteen at Wellingborough was upstairs, above the offices, and in front of the toilets; one of the staff was called Gladys. The former Booking Office at the depot was by then the Manager's Office. Brian Mills was the first Manager, followed by Bob Coote and finally David Shadbolt. David had the unpleasant task of closing the depot, which came as a surprise as United Counties had spent much money on upgrading its facilities.

The Social Club held events at the Railway Club in Broad Green, Wellingborough. Weekends away were arranged to Europe, and the places visited included France, Austria and Belgium. These trips had two designated drivers and used a company vehicle.

Buses used a lay-by outside Wellingborough Technical College as a bus station. Sometimes, however, all the bays were full and buses were left in the main carriageway. This caused confusion as cars had to drive round them. In many instances when the bus bays emptied the bus was marooned on its own in the middle of the road, and the passengers had to negotiate the cars to reach it.

Drivers were co-opted to drive at Silverstone Circuit for the Grand Prix. Six buses were used to take the marshals around the track. Buses left

Graham Truett and David King. *Mick Hedge collection*

Northampton at 5.00am and returned about midnight. One year Des Banyard made international news by accidentally taking a corner too tightly and one of the back wheels landed in the gravel. The racing was held up until Des and his bus were rescued.

Wages in 1982 were £1.51 per hour for crew drivers, £1.82 for OMO drivers and £1.49 for conductors, all these being for a 39-hour week.

Mick was asked by Jeannie Warwick to work at Northampton two weeks before Wellingborough closed. This worked out well, and as a result he was offered a job at Greyfriars Bus Station as a driver, and worked here until he retired in 2001. One Northampton driver, Martin Kelly, was well-known by his prominent sideburns, while another, Frank Bailey, was the quickest eater, clearing his meal in 3 minutes flat. Before retiring Mick used to drive the Northampton staff bus, either on the 04.00 to 11.30 or 15.00 to midnight shift. He also sometimes drove coaches; he remembers that Inspector Cox used to hide behind a tree near Scratchwood Services and jump out at unsuspected drivers as they passed by.

Later in his career Mike was outstationed in the Wellingborough area again, working out of the Raunds, Wymington and Chowns Mill outstations. Also working at Chowns Mill were Norman Soden, Mick Dunn, Bev Watson and Tony Winch.

Since retiring, Mick has been collecting much data

Kevin Baxter and Glen Stewart. *Mick Hedge collection*

and information about United Counties, some of it from the closure of the Main Works in Northampton, including accident insurance photographs of vehicles and components that failed in service.

Mick remembers two of his accidents. One was when an unfortunate reveller fell under the back wheels of his bus in Northampton outside the Abingdon Street cinema and died at the scene. Fortunately police and a nurse saw the accident.

The other accident occurred when he reversed a bus into another one coming round a corner. Mick was somewhere he should not have been and the other bus, driven by Kevin, was going a bit fast. Both buses had to go to Northampton to be repaired.

One day Mick was involved in filming for BBC's *Keeping up Appearances*. He was on a spare turn and was asked to take a bus out to a Northampton location, where one of the characters was supposed to drive it.

John Appleton

John joined the railways when he left school in 1949. He became a cleaner and quickly a 'passed cleaner' then a locomotive fireman at the British Railways sheds at Wellingborough. This was a heavy freight locomotive depot and the engines at that time were mostly Stanier 8Fs or Garretts on the heavy coal trains to London. All men had to do two years of National Service in the 1950s, so John joined the transport companies of the Royal Armaments Supply Corps and worked with the REME

Len Rowell, who taught Mick Hedge to conduct. *Mick Hedge collection*

Norman Soden and Derrick Warboys. *Mick Hedge collection*

in Germany and Korea.

After this service he joined the United Counties Engineering Department on the early and late running shift at Wellingborough, working with his mate Ted Clayson doing all kinds of running repair work. Les King was the Mechanical Foreman at Wellingborough, a very nice and knowledgeable man who would always help and advise them. Working in the garage, he was able to drive all the buses around, and with this and his Army experience in 1956 he took his driving instruction with the Depot Instructor, the helpful Ron Garon. On his test he was carrying not only Ron but also the Foreman Driver, Frank Chambers, and the MOT Examiner, Mr Stock. John can remember that the test bus, a Bristol K Type double-decker, was numbered 785 and registered ERP 605. John remembers that he also drove it on his first passenger-carrying service the following Saturday.

Driving was confined to non-shift days and holiday times. Wellingborough Depot was very short of drivers in those days, so on his days off John was usually driving on service. When he transferred to the day shift, he had more time for driving. Shifts were for five days with two days off, but not at weekends, due to the high demand for work to be done then. Les King used to have John in on Saturday mornings, cleaning down the benches, the inspection pits and all the tools they used. The garage area they used was kept immaculate.

United Counties buses mainly had Bristol or Gardner engines. The Bristols would leak permanently and would not use reclaimed oil, whereas the Gardners were leak-free and would use it.

In 1960 John moved over to full-time driving, which he enjoyed because he could keep clean and tidy.

Olney was an outstation of Wellingborough in those days; three crews worked from there and they had two double-deckers. The crews included Dennis Tomlin, whose son opened a barber's shop in the town. Some of the buses that worked there were 831, 832,

John Appleton with a Bristol J Type bus. *John Appleton collection*

837 and 838, which were Bristol KS types. The outstation was a former cowshed, which could just house the buses. However, when both buses were 8-footers it was a tight squeeze to get them in; one had to bounce over the stone that held the doors when they were closed. Getting to Olney could be tricky in snowy weather. However, the buses were fitted by Ron Evans with tyres from the Avon Tyre Company, which seemed to be better in snowy weather. Olney drivers worked on the 407 route, which in those days only went to Wellingborough. In later years, when Olney closed, the 407 was mainly Bozeat to Kettering via Wollaston, Wellingborough and Isham, with occasional trips to

Olney outstation. *Roger Warwick collection*

455 on service at Bedford. *John Appleton collection*

Olney. Olney was also served by the 128 service from Bedford to Northampton, which was crewed from Bedford, Yardley Hastings and Northampton, but not Olney.

John remembers that another outstation was at Addington Road, Irthlingborough. He remembers using the engineers van on a Sunday to take out a Mr Valentine, who could not drive, to collect the

The helpful Johnny Ashelford with 431. *John Appleton collection*

money from the safe at this depot and take it to the Midland Bank in Kettering. Talking of the money, he remembers that the money bus at Wellingborough used to go down and park outside the bank – no security in those days – and the money was taken in by a number of staff to be credited to the United Counties account. The bus was left in the bus bay outside, blocking any service buses.

Workers' buses were a large part of United Counties work in the 1950s and 1960s. Corby steelworks had two double-decker buses from Wellingborough and two from Rushden for each shift. The late-night and early buses were driven by the same crews, who were supposed to sleep at Wellingborough Depot between duties. Some would, but others would go home and come back later. The Rushden buses were a saloon and a double-decker; the saloon bus would be left in Corby until the end of the shift, while the other came home with both crews.

When a driver had been with the company for more than three years he would be invited to drive the coaches on scheduled express and excursion traffic. John jumped at the chance, as he was 'cab happy' by that time. John remembers that the original Wellingborough coaches, Bristol LWL 'Queen Marys', were numbered 378 and 379. They were only registered for the summer, and were parked in the back corner of the depot in the winter. They were covered with old destination blinds sewn together,

which were taken off in the spring and the buses repainted before use. Later coaches, after John left Wellingborough, included 263, 278 and 288, which were Bristol REs, and 203, a Bristol MW. John took two Leyland Titans to the dump at Bedford on their retirement.

The main scheduled coach services were to Cheltenham, Portsmouth and Bournemouth. The Cheltenham services were run by Kettering Depot, with Wellingborough providing the duplicates, while the other two were run by Royal Blue (the NBC company, not Royal Blue coaches of Pytchley). On his first runs, John was supposed to follow the other coaches. Unfortunately the Royal Blue coaches had six-cylinder engines and he only had a five, which made him slower. The other coaches would sometimes wait for him at scheduled stops, but others would go to, say, Newbury and Andover when going to Portsmouth or Bournemouth and leave him to it. They were supposed to meet up in Winchester, but the other driver had already gone when John arrived. Fortunately he was able to get a local Royal Blue driver to pilot him to the coast, which was on that driver's way home.

The first coach he drove was 455, a Bristol LS, on a trip to Cheltenham. The Kettering driver that day was Johnny Ashelford, who showed John the ropes and waited for him when he got left behind. John thought it was nice of him to do this and made the trip a pleasure. Another of the coach drivers, later on, was Mick Rainbow.

John is now a leading light in the Chelveston Vehicle Preservation Group, an involvement that started in 1974. Within the group they have a United Counties Bristol J Type coach, a United Counties LWL coach, a Lincolnshire Bristol SU coach, three Bristol LH buses and an Eastern National Bristol KS double-decker. John owns one of the LH buses, which was an Eastern Counties contribution to an NBC stand at the Motor Show. It even has NBC moquette on the seats. The other two are Southern National and Lincolnshire.

These buses usually attend local and national rallies around the country. One, LWL CNH 862, was used by local bus couple Mr and Mrs David Shadbolt when they married. It also went to Bedford to be involved in the retirement of Dick Watson. Some of the buses also went to United Counties depot open days at Bedford, Luton and Milton Keynes. John goes to Chelveston two or three days a week and says that it feels like going back to work again.

He still likes to ride the local buses and occasionally sees someone he knows. Today's vehicles are sleeker and faster, but to John the half-cab of a K Type Bristol with a five-cylinder Gardner diesel engine throbbing away and a speedometer that cuts out at 28mph brings back the memories!

John, Peter and Tony at the Chelveston Vehicle Preservation Group headquarters with 428. *John Appleton collection*

Bill Mors

Bill Mors and Richard Haseldine are two of four mates who used to be good at having fun together.

John Appleton, Pat Palmer, John Willis and Brian Barton. *Mick Hedge collection*

Kevin Pinney, Mick White, Dick Gayton, Richard Haseldine and Bill Mors. *Mick Hedge collection*

Most of their exploits are unrepeatable or unprintable, but they enjoyed themselves!

One day Bill was driving a Wellingborough town service to the railway station and back. At the station there was a rest period before the return and, not having many passengers, Eddie Brown, the conductor, went round the station to see if any more were lurking in corners or in the tea room. Not aware of this, the bell rang on time and Bill headed back to the town centre. When the passengers wanted to get off they rang the bell, so Bill did not know he was on his own. He picked up in town, then headed back to the station. On the way down Mill Road he noticed Eddie walking the other way, having a stroll back to the depot.

Apparently Eddie was always on the look-out for potential customers, and more than once had his head caught in the folding doors of an FLF as the driver set off. The driver would look in his nearside mirror and see Eddie's head sticking out of the door.

Bill worked at Wellingborough Depot and transferred to Northampton when Wellingborough closed. At the time of writing he drives for First Northampton.

David Shadbolt

After a reorganisation in 1985 (see also Chapters 1 and 13), David moved north to become the District Manager for Wellingborough and Northampton, based in the old Booking Office at Wellingborough Depot. He remembers that Rod Davies was the Northampton Depot Superintendent at the time.

One of his first jobs was to evaluate the operations and to help with reviewing his network in preparation for the deregulation of bus services. He worked with Rod Davies, Paul De Santis, Steve Loveridge, Ray Ramsey and Ben Colson to achieve this; they were a good team and he thought highly of them.

Part of the preparation was a review of overheads, and it was decided that United Counties in Northamptonshire had more depot capacity than was sustainable commercially. Therefore one depot had to close – Northampton, Kettering, Corby or Wellingborough. David and the District Engineer, Peter Grimes, were summoned to Head Office and told by John Tate that Wellingborough would close. One of the hardest things David has ever had to do was to go back to Wellingborough and tell everyone. It was a very difficult time for them all; some staff were redeployed to Kettering, Bedford and Northampton, while others left. The worst time was when one of the conductors went home and was found dead in his garage next day; this memory has stayed with David all his working career and he will never forget it. The Wellingborough staff still respect David for the way he dealt with the run-down and closure, trying to help them all he could.

David had a flair for marketing and this was to give him a boost to his career later on. He was often in the local papers helping to raise money for various charities and was often seen at local carnivals selling the company's services and raising more money.

David Shadbolt teaches Lucie Warboys to drive a bus during a school visit to Wellingborough Depot. *United Counties News*

Ron Evans

Ron has never worked for any of the bus companies dealt with in this book even though he has worked in the depots at Wellingborough and Kettering for many years. Ron fits tyres and works for the Michelin tyre company. Without his essential work, the buses would not be safe to go out on service and would definitely not pass their MOTs. Other depots will have their equivalent of Ron to do this work for them. The tyre fitters work closely with the maintenance teams at each depot. Ron can easily be seen at Kettering, as he is always dressed in a bright orange uniform.

Caroline Cleaveley

Being born in November 1956 at the Barratt Maternity Hospital, Northampton, next door to Houghton Road Works and within half a mile of Derngate Bus Station of United Counties, I would have seen and heard buses all round me, but they made no impression. Living up at Winchester Road, Delapre, Mum, Dad, my grandmother and I would have used the Northampton Transport services, which started at the end of the road and took us into town. Here again I have no recollections.

When we lived in Rushden, Mum used to walk or push me to Higham Ferrers and Rushden as a daily event. Our daily walks would have meant

being around most of Rushden's allocation of vehicles. If we went to Wellingborough or further afield we would have gone in the car.

My memories start when we moved to Mears Ashby in 1960. This village was the halfway point for service 401 between Wellingborough and Northampton, calling at Doddington, Earls Barton, Sywell, Overstone and Moulton, and wending its way down the Kettering Road to Abington Square, then on to Derngate Bus Station. As Mears Ashby was a sleepy village of 200 houses, there was not much excitement for a four-year-old, so the daily passing of these big green buses became a way of telling the time. I always seemed to wake to the sound of the early workers' bus making its way up the narrow 'Tin Barn Road' (local name) to Sywell Airport and Phillips Electricals/London Carriers.

Most buses crossed at Mears Ashby. Therefore we had a bus to Northampton and Wellingborough each morning at about 8.00, 9.30 and 11.30, and in the afternoon and evening at 1.30, 4.30, 6.30, 8.30, 9.30 and 10.30. On Saturdays there was a bus at 11.00pm but I rarely heard that, as I was in bed by 8.00pm and asleep by 10.00pm. The Sunday service ran during the afternoon so that all the busmen could sleep in or go to church in the morning.

The Saturday late bus stays in my Dad's memory for ever. His birthday is in the middle of November, and the council had dug a hole in the road by the bus stop opposite our house. In those days holes were guarded by acetylene lamps lit daily. The night before his birthday our cat Margaret had gone to investigate the hole and the lights at the same time as the late bus, which frightened her and killed her as she tried to get away from it. Dad did not find her until next morning and his first job on his birthday was to bury his cat. Suffice to say that he did not have a good birthday that year.

Service 401 was mainly operated by double-deckers and the occasional single-decker supplied by Wellingborough Depot, initially Bristol KSWs and LDs. The Bristol FS took over from the KSWs and we would occasionally have an FLF on balancing turns back from Northampton. Some buses were supplied by Northampton or Rushden garages, normally only at weekends or if Wellingborough was short. The single-deckers were mainly Bristol MW or LS variants and we did have the odd visit by 203, which was an MW coach. On a few occasions a bus from Luton, Bedford

**The 'Monkey Bus', 771, leaving Derngate for Wellingborough
on the 401 service.** *Policy Transport Photos of Allestree, author's collection*

or Kettering would appear on a running-in turn from Houghton Road.

My memories at this time include the following vehicles: Bristol LDs 502, 509, 511, 515, 531, 533, 535, 542 and 559; Bristol FSs 612, 615, 650, 651, 652, 653 (very occasionally as a Rushden bus), 673, 681, 682, 683, 713 and 714 (very occasionally as Rushden buses); and Bristol FLFs 632, 633, 634, 697, 719 and 720.

I remember the KSWs well, due to their staggered seats upstairs, which made life interesting if you were up by the window. Wellingborough Garage had quite a few, including the now preserved 964.

My memories of travel were mainly with Mum to Wellingborough during the summer holidays to shop, coming home with Dad by car, and Saturday trips to Northampton, including a visit to Adams's Bakery Café, downstairs, which was decorated as an airliner, or to the Wimpy Bar in Abington Street. The highlight for Mum was a visit to Adnitts in the Drapery, and for me it was to stand in Derngate Bus Station watching the activity while we had a cup of tea from the Snack Bar. The oldest buses, mainly

KSWs, seemed to work on the 321/322 Quarry Road workings. This seemed quite a romantic destination, as I dreamed of the bus turning round inside an old quarry with workers changing shift. However, the reality was mainly young Mums and children.

Service 401 always seemed to go from bay 2, which we seemed to share with the 329 for Moulton. These tended to go out just before ours, so the 401 bus would be over in the layover bays by the Café. When the 329 had gone the driver of our bus would start it up and rev it for all he was worth, creating a very unhealthy smog in the process. He would then back it to the given bay, where the conductor would guide him in. Bay 1 was invariably for buses on the 402/3/4 routes to Wellingborough and beyond. These were mainly FLFs on the 402, with a mixture on the rest. Rushden buses could be seen on the 403 and 404 routes, being mainly its FSs; its FLFs 635 and 636 were rarely seen on these routes.

One interesting fact was that the bus station was the emergency exit for the Green Room of the Royal Theatre next door, the metal stairs coming down behind the buffet. Actors could thus rush off stage, change and run down the steps to catch their last bus home.

All the buses used to back into the bays. This was all right for the majority of back-loaders, but when the Bristol FLFs and later single-decker Bristol RELLs were used, this became a safety problem. Talking of safety, in the 1960s and 1970s the travelling public did not seem to mind being dropped off amongst manoeuvring buses and coaches. Each passenger, and bus driver, looked after his or her own safety and I never heard of anyone being run over.

To me, Derngate Bus Station was the centre of the bus universe. The building was impressive from the approach, the offices and Café making up the front. The bus entry was to the east, passing the layover bays outside and the more interesting bit, the coach bays, on entering the building. At that time United Counties coaches were mainly the new Bristol RELHs 250-276, and Bristol MW 203 was seen occasionally too. The main route seemed to be Nottingham to London, although we were more interested in the coach from Cheltenham, as grandma used to visit on that one from Stroud.

Some Saturdays the coach bays were full of vehicles from all parts of Britain: Midland Red, Yelloway, Southdown, East Kent, Royal Blue (the Western National not the Pytchley version), Jeff's Coaches, York's Coaches, and Wesley Tours coaches (used to duplicate). Other coaches making occasional visits were Ribble/Standerwick, United, Eastern Counties and South Midlands. Other bus companies had joint services with United Counties and the occasional Oxford or Eastern Counties bus was seen. I believe that very occasional visits were made by Northampton Transport buses, but I never saw one in the temple of Derngate.

The west door of the bus station was the exit, and had a pedestrian walkway separated from the bus road; however, quite often the buses and passengers would come out together along the roadway. The main booking office was by the exit, being near the town, and was strategically placed as all bus users would have gone past it.

An unusual event was the arrival of the papers. The *Chronicle & Echo* would be distributed by bus, the van driving around each bay. Each village would have a convenient bus stop for the delivery person's house, where the conductor would throw the papers as the bus passed. Buses would also carry parcels, which you collected from the bus as it arrived. In later years

At the 1999 reunion of Wellingborough bus people, the two stars were Jack Waite and Eddie Brown.
Stagecoach United Counties News

I bought a bus blind from Houghton Road Works, which arrived on the 401.

When I transferred to school in Wellingborough, I travelled daily by United Counties 401 service at 8.00am and returned on the 4.00pm service. A school bus was provided, which only called at John Lea School in the morning, starting at about 8.15am from Mears Ashby. In later years this was invariably a Wellingborough Bristol RELL, either 334, 335, 336 or 342. The school bus in the evening running in front of the 4.00pm service could be used, but as I was bullied I travelled on the normal service most often. To avoid mixing with the bullies I invariably caught this bus by Swanspool Gardens or even in Market Street if I ran quickly enough. As I lived more than 3 miles from school I had a termly bus pass, which could also be used at weekends. This was very useful in later years.

In the early 1970s the old LDs were confined to Wellingborough town services, replacing the KSWs, and new flat-fronted vehicles arrived, being the aforementioned RELLs and new Bristol VRs. Wellingborough only had one in the early years, 757, but a while later it was followed by 771; this was special to me, as it was the 'Monkey Bus'. This was the first advert bus I had seen; it was painted yellow and purple with 'Jungle Book' characters, and was an advert for a local garage. It is quite ironic that this company now has a car sales and repair garage housed in the old bus depot in St Johns Street, Wellingborough. Being very nervous in my early teens I was afraid of this bus, as it was unusual; however, having travelled to Northampton on it once it then became my favourite.

It was during the early 1970s that my interest in

buses flourished. I would catch the 8.00am bus out of the village on a Saturday morning and end up in far-flung destinations such as Aylesbury (by train and bus from Luton) and Peterborough by way of Northampton to Kettering on the 256, then on the joint run via Thrapston. This latter service was out on a United Counties FS6B and back with an Eastern Counties FS6G. The drivers preferred the Eastern Counties buses, as they were much faster; I believe they had Gardners instead of Bristol engines.

It was also during this time that I became acquainted with a couple of conductors from Wellingborough Depot – Charlie Haines, who lived in Mears Ashby and soon retired to become the village postman, and Eddie Brown from Wellingborough. Most of the others were friendly but I found these two more interesting to speak to.

I was afraid of one of the two conductresses at Wellingborough. She appeared not to stand any nonsense on 'her' bus, and I would always sit still and not move until it was time to get off. She later became a driver on RELLs and I was always afraid of her then too!

Charlie Haines used to tell me stories from his days as a conductor, which I should have taped, and now regret having forgotten. Eddie was much more an outgoing character and would invite me out for the day to help him by operating the doors manually on the back-loaders and by ringing the bell. I soon learned the bell code: 1 = stop, 2 = start, 3 = full, 4 = get round here as soon as possible, because I have trouble back here and need your help!

The passengers did not seem to mind me doing this work and some commented that I was a good trainee. I tried to get a job conducting in the summer holidays, but United Counties had stopped taking on occasional student staff at that time. The main problem we encountered was with the Inspectors. Eddie Brown would give me a sixpenny ticket if an Inspector got on and I would get off at the last stop on the run and wander about until Eddie and his driver went out again. If we were working from Wellingborough Depot I would wait up the road and they would pick me up there.

When we went into Derngate I had to pretend to be a passenger until we had left and were halfway down the road. As a result of this I learned the routes to Irthlingborough, Raunds, Rushden, Kettering, Bozeat and Northampton. The longest run was to Odell and Harrold on the River Ouse. This was a one-off Sunday run out and back. We would meet up with a bus from Bedford in case any passengers wanted to go through, although invariably none seemed to.

Occasionally the school bus would have an unusual vehicle. As well as 203 we occasionally had RELH 263, then the former Birch Brothers coaches in the 170 and 190 series. Later on RELHs 278 and 288 would appear. I found the Birch coaches were

plush in comparison to the United Counties ones, and I would get excited when 170 turned up on the 401. The most comfortable vehicle we had on the 401 was one of the Eastern National semi-automatics FLFs (I think it was AVX ???G). Coach seats in a double-decker were great, but not very practical, and I only rode on it once. In later years the Bristol VRs began to take over from the older buses. I must admit I lost interest as I felt their flat fronts made them look boring compared to the half-cabs, and I found the vibration on the RELLs was not to my liking.

When driver-only buses came in I could not go out with Eddie any more, and exams interfered with my days out, which brought an end to my unofficial United Counties conducting. However, I made occasional visits (mainly at the weekend) to Houghton Road Works to see what was going on, and these were fine as long as the duty foreman was amenable. 'Don't fall down the pits and be careful. Report when you go,' was all that was said, and I could then have an hour to wander round. Here I found buses that never seemed to go out on the road. Were they someone's pets that only went out on high days and holidays, or mechanically not good? I suspect the latter. United Counties always had buses off-licence in the winter, but some seemed to stay at Houghton Road for years. One vehicle to go off-license seemed to be FS 653 from Rushden.

At Houghton Road Works I was able to see some of the buses brought in from other companies at times of shortage. I remember the FLF coaches, RTTs from Western National, the former Luton Corporation buses and, in later years, those strange yellow buses with only one passenger seat. These were the training buses that used to be FS 713-718. I knew 713-715 as they were Rushden buses, and 717 and 718 were Northampton buses, but there was also this 'foreign' bus, 716, from down south at Luton. On a later visit the yard was full of white coaches, which I was told were being bought for the new National Express network.

It was at this time that I decided to buy an old bus and turn it into a caravan to live in. I went along to Houghton Road Works, saw training bus 714 in the yard, photographed it and made an approach by letter to buy it. However, I could not afford it, and have often kicked myself for not buying it then by taking out a loan. However, on my next visit to see it it had gone; the new fangled Stagecoach company, from up north, had bought United Counties and had wafted 714 to Perth for further use.

It was not until 2006 that I found that 714 had not been broken up and was nearly intact as withdrawn at Lochalmond in Fife. I checked on her condition and visited her later that year. Since then I have been trying to buy her again, now that I can afford it, and restore her to recreate the routes of my childhood. I am determined to not let her go a second time!

Around the mid-1970s I had another shock. The Derngate Bus Station, my Mecca for buses, was coming down and a new one was being built on the other side of the town centre. Having learned to drive in 1975, I rarely used buses to go to town, but when I did I found Greyfriars Bus Station very unfriendly, cold and dark, with no atmosphere. Where were the buffet and café where you could watch for your bus? Passengers had to be controlled and kept away from the buses until they had arrived and were ready to board.

Since that time I have only been able to view United Counties from afar. I missed out on the Ford mini- and Bedford midi-buses, the Leyland Olympians, the RM phenomenon in Corby and Bedford, and the majority of the Leyland Nationals (Wellingborough only had one or two when I left the area). I was, however, glad to see that some of my old friends had made it to the Stagecoach takeover. I have since been collecting any photographs I can get my hands on, mainly from the 1960-80 period. I have also talked to the owners of the various preserved vehicles and commissioned a painting and prints of United Counties vehicles. The original was in Steve Loveridge's office at Rothersthorpe Avenue when I last saw it in 2008.

I am glad that the depots at Wellingborough and Rushden are still in use, though neither has seen a bus for ages. The only local depot that I still recognise is at Kettering (still with United Counties buses in it). I am looking forward to the centenary of Wellingborough buses in 2013, and hopefully some of my favourite FS vehicles (including 651, 714 and 715) can take part, although since writing that FS 715 has been burned out in a fire.

Isn't it a shame that other old friends are not about, especially 203, 263, 650, 681, 682, 632, 633, 634 and 697, and maybe one of the LDs? On a personal note, I am glad that one of the Eastern National semi-coaches is preserved somewhere in East Anglia. Preserved vehicles from my era include 964, 252, 260 (still in use in East Anglia), 273, 278 (still in use in North Wales), 279 (broken up for spares in 2008), 651 (in bits), 712, 714, 715 (see above), 757, 767, 774 and a few of the Bristol RELLs.

David Morris-Smith

David did not work for United Counties, but the buses had a huge impact on his childhood in Wellingborough, as he explains.

My earliest memories are during the Second World War. In the 1940s, while at infants school, I used to walk home along 'Outlaw Lane', which runs along the back of the old fairground behind the bus garage. At this time St Johns Street Garage was relatively new. I used to peer through the fence to see the lines of

retired single-decker Leyland Lions of the 1920s.

Later in life I went to Wellingborough School, where I met my best friend Brian Peters. Brian was very interesting because his father was a local ticket inspector from Irthlingborough. Brian unfortunately did not follow his father, but became a Methodist minister instead.

We formed a group with another boy, and called ourselves the 'Mid-Northants Omnibus Spotters Club'. We even had our own stationery printed, which was quite something in 1948. Using this, we circulated all the major bus companies in the United Kingdom asking for complimentary copies of their timetables. These we found were fantastic volumes, with Midland Red requiring four books!

We used these timetables to see how far we could get from Wellingborough in a day by fare-stage services. This gave us a source of innocent fun and was great for teaching us geography. It was possible to get to such far-flung places as Manchester and Taunton in only one day.

In the summer United Counties and Royal Blue (Western/Southern National) ran a daily service from Northampton to Bournemouth. As an example of how keen we must have been, after school we used to cycle over to Houghton Road Garage in Northampton where the Royal Blue coach was kept overnight, after depositing passengers at Derngate Bus Station. This bus was usually a beautiful Bristol, with its fantastic side window, destination blind and roof rack being the ultimate in coach design at that time. The two services left Northampton and Bournemouth at 10.00am and arrived at their destinations at about 3.00pm. Sometimes we had ridden the 20 miles only to see one of our local United Counties coaches on the service, which caused us disappointment.

The Tilling Group companies were our favourites and we used to 'go nuts' to see a 'foreign' bus. Kettering had a service to Peterborough, which was run jointly with Eastern Counties, and these buses had unique wooden destination blinds. At that time Olney had a service from Bedford provided by Eastern National; this was before Bedford and surrounding areas (Western Division) were taken over by United Counties. Midland Red had a fare-stage service from Northampton to Shrewsbury, which ran via Birmingham and started at the Mayorhold in Northampton instead of the bus station.

At other times we used to cycle the 19 miles to Towcester to sit by the A5 road to catch all the London-bound summer services. Included in these were vehicles from such companies as SMT, Standerwick and Scout, PMT, Crosville, Midland Red and all the Birmingham private coaches. These were the 'golden days' of bus and coach travel in this country.

I left school in 1951 and that was the end of the group. However, I never lost my interest, even when

I did my National Service from 1954 to 1956.

I remember that Eastern Coach Works (ECW) had a small unit at Irthlingborough, which was used after the war to re-body old chassis from all the Tilling companies. I remember visiting most days, with my friends, as they finished three or four vehicles a week. This we found was wonderful, especially as vehicles were freshly painted and left outside for collection. Company vehicles we remember were from United, Southern Vectis and Thames Valley, all being names I still recall with affection.

Another of our interests was the Associated Motorways group of companies, of which United Counties was one. We once had a treasured trip to Cheltenham, where we revelled in the masses of Black & White coaches that we saw.

I still have friends who used to work for United Counties and one of these was John Thompson, who worked at Daventry.

Val Everard in her counting house, this time at Kettering in 2007 having moved from Wellingborough on its closure.
Stagecoach East collection

Val Everard

Val has worked for the company for more than 40 years, first at Wellingborough, as a cashier, then at Kettering. She remembers that the conductors had to put the money in the safe, and her job was to take it on the bank bus to the Midland Bank. In those days she stood in the queue and had to wait while it was counted. Nowadays a security firm deals with all financial matters.

In 1981 Val worked part-time in Kettering on Thursdays, to do the overs and unders in the wages. The wages were counted out into packets and noted in the wages book. The pay cheques used to come over from Northampton. The job of wages clerk ceased when computers were used, and now all money is paid into the bank and wages are dealt with at Stockport.

Val then became a detailer, doing the wages with Vivian Thompson, but is now a cashier again. Other jobs she does are taking in private hire money, petrol cash receipts and dealing with the petty cash. She also produces daily

information for Brian Hadden and the Stockport Stagecoach Accounts Office.

From the Wellingborough Archive

All photographs from the Mick Hedge collection unless otherwise credited.

Mick Perry

Top left: **Richard and Mrs Gayton**

Above: **Kevin Pinney and Eddie Brown**

Left: **Stan Horner and Joe Parnell**

Above: **Phil Sharpe**

Left: **Vince Cleary (background) and Jim McClusky**

Gladys from the canteen

Dick Gayton with John and Mrs Tapp

Tony Townsend, Brian Barton, Ray Ramsey and Steve Chambers

Al Williams and Brian Silby

Wellingborough cleaners

Sid Waples

George Meacher

Richard Vanhoof and Steve Goulden

Jim Kerrigan

Graham Mitchell

Vince Cleary, Marshall Cook and Colin Palmer

Ron Sanders

John and Mrs Neville

Frank and Chrissie Howell

Trevor Edwards

Kevin Pinney in his other uniform!

At Wellingborough Railwaymen's Club, Broad Green – see anyone you recognise? *Dick Watson collection*

Above: **Harold Chambers and 612.** *John Appleton collection*

Right: **Joshi and 559.** *John Appleton collection*

22
Yardley Hastings

Yardley Hastings outstation. *Roger Warwick collection*

Yardley Hastings was an out-station of Bedford.

Douglas Moore and Glenis Deer

Douglas is from Dovercourt, near Harwich, in Essex. He applied for a job as a conductor with Eastern National in 1936 and due to a transfer ended up in Bedford in 1938, where they were short-staffed. Douglas was part-time at Harwich, and his boss was a Mr Vincent. He remembers a busmen's trip to London, with lunch in Epping Forest and a show at the London Palladium.

Douglas was originally allocated digs in Ashburnham Road, Bedford, owned by a fellow conductor who charged him £1 a week rent. After a while he changed digs and moved to Bower Street. Some of the Bedford staff were given nicknames, and Douglas's was 'Cuddly Dudley'. One driver was called 'Side Saddle'. Douglas used to visit the house of Bob McDonald, a Bedford driver, to have a cup of Oxo, and while there he met his future wife.

At this time some of the conductors would issue 1,500 tickets a day. They were responsible for the health and safety of the passengers and had to do waybills. Bedford originally had Bell punch machines before Setrights were used. One of the conductors was dismissed for drilling a small hole in his machine and defrauding the company. Some conductors used a whistle to call on their drivers when the bus was reversing.

One day a conductor went to the Bridge Street snooker rooms in Northampton and played a professional. He won. The next day he was set upon and all his company money taken.

Maurice Jewitt was in charge at Bedford, and was very strict. Douglas was friends with Stan Burton and used to take tomatoes in for him during the growing season. Joe Clough was another driver; he had served in the First World War and his regular conductor was Joe Swine. Mr and Mrs Woods were a driver and conductress together. Les Bidewell was the Senior Office Clerk, and Harry Hucknall was an Inspector. Richard Askew and Ray Ramsey are also remembered from the Bedford offices.

A company called Union Jack used to provide buses from Kempston to Bedford, but was bought out by Eastern National.

Douglas was assigned to Yardley Hastings outstation in 1939 and worked as a driver on the route from Northampton to Cambridge until his retirement in 1980. The original Northampton terminus was outside St John's railway station, but after 1952 services were re-routed to Derngate. Originally two crews were based at Cambridge for this service, but in later years it was covered from Northampton, Yardley and Bedford. At Croxton the local landowner used to give crews poultry and cigarettes at Christmas. The service was taken over by United Counties when Eastern National was reorganised, and became route 128.

Yardley staff would take their turns on Bedford town services. They also used to shunt buses late at night. One night a mechanic was called out to Douglas's bus when the air system had water in it. Other staff included conductress Mrs Minney and conductor Reg Coleman

The depot at Yardley was a shed that accommodated two 7ft 6in buses but only one if it was 8 feet wide. When Douglas accidentally scratched the mudguard on his bus he was disciplined by Mr Jewitt. Northampton crews would not put a bus in the shed in case they damaged them. The first crew had to get out their bus at 6.00am and when the last bus came back at 11.00pm it was put to bed and the staff walked home. The shed also was a stable for a horse, and some staff used to be afraid of it. Buses were routed into the shed by the Post Office end of the village, and had to reverse out of it.

During the war, from 1940, Douglas joined up as

Douglas Moore receives his 25-year award from John Hargreaves.
Douglas Moore collection

a cook in the Bedfordshire & Hertfordshire Regiment. One of his senior officers was Major Wells of the well-known local brewing family. He became a prisoner of war in Burma, working on the notorious Burma Railway. When he returned in 1945 he had six months leave and recovery time before returning to the buses. His pay for five years of Army service was £111.

The Northampton area was run by Norman Maycock. Yardley men were included in the Christmas raffles held at Northampton. Staff dances were held at the Corn Hall in Bedford, with tickets at 2s 6d each or 4s 6d for a couple.

Bedford buses from Northampton used bay 12, which was near the canteen. Some late passengers used to run across the bus station to catch their bus, and the drivers would see their regulars coming and wait for them; some drivers would stop for late passengers in Derngate itself, although Douglas would not do this. The other service on their route was the 129 for Olney or Newport Pagnell. As a summer trip, six double-deckers would leave Derngate for the river at Bedford.

On retirement, Douglas worked for 13 years driving for local undertaker D. Hollowell & Sons, driving cars to Coventry, Rugby and Hemel Hempstead.

George's daughter Glenis Deer remembers that she and her Mum used to get the bus to Yardley and take Dad his dinner. Sometimes it was a hotpot, which he would share with Charlie Cox, his conductor, before going back to work. Glenis used to go to the children's Christmas parties at the Corn Hall in Bedford.

John Kelly

John now works as a driver at Bedford, but started his career as a conductor at Yardley Hastings. He worked there for four years and remembers drivers such as Herbie Little.

While still a conductor, John was working with Jeff Ingram on a 70-seater Bristol FLF when they needed to reverse by a pub. For speed John went out of the back emergency door and forgot to shut it. He was guiding Jeff back when Jeff was distracted by a sports car doing an unusual manoeuvre round him; he kept coming back and the open emergency door knocked John off his feet and under the reversing bus. He was shaken but fortunately not hurt.

Just before we closed for press Mr and Mrs Watson from Bedford sent me this additional photograph, showing their father's bus (see page 20).

Appendix

List of known members of staff, depot by depot

Key

App	Apprentice	DC	Detail Clerk	PA	Personal Assistant
Asst	Assistant	DE	Depot Engineer	S	Superintendent
BB	Body-builder	DI	Driving Instructor	SBB	Skilled Body-builder
BM	Body-maker	DM	Depot Manager	Sec	Secretary
C	Conductor	DS	Depot Superintendent	SF	Skilled Fitter
CC	Chief Clerk	DTM	Depot Traffic Manager	St	Storeman
CHE	Chargehand Electrician	E	Engineer(ing)	Super	Superintendent
CHF	Chargehand Fitter	El	Electrician	T	Telephonist
Ck	Clerk	EM	Engineering Manager	TM	Traffic Manager
Cl	Cleaner	F	Fitter	TR	Traffic Records
Cont	Controller	FC	Father Christmas	TS	Traffic Superintendent
Cs	Conductress	GM	General Manager	TSh	Travel Shop
CSO	Customer Service Officer	I	Inspector	UCE	United Counties Engineering
Csr	Cashier	MD	Managing Director	VC	Vehicle cleaner
D	Driver	MF	Mechanical Foreman	WC	Wages Clerk
DAB	Dial-a-Bus	MSC	Map System Designer		
		OM	Operations Manager		
		P	Painter		

Aylesbury
Atkins, Q. (Cs)
Berry, A. F. (C, F)
Connoly, J. (FC)
Cumming, G. (S)
Durbin, G. (Service Section)
Ewer, D. A.
Fleming, J. (D)
Frost, L. R. (D)
Frost, S. E. (D)
Galvin, D. (C)
Hawkins, T. H. (I)
Howard, G. (D)
Jeffery, P. (D)
Koiston, A. H. (VC)
Lawrence, W. A. (D)
Moore, N. (DE)
Mortimer, F. H. G.
Norgate, T. J. (F)
Pantling, F. F. (C)
Phillips, W. (D)
Renilson, N. (S)
Sales, W. (C)
Simonds, A. E. (C)
Simpson, A. C. O. (C)
Smith, A. W. (I)
Smith, B. (S)
Spittles, P. (SF)
Stainton, W. (F)
Stone, B. (I)

Stone, H. V.
Swain, H. J. (D)
Swan, R. F. (MF)
Thomas, W. (C)
Todd, H. H. (D)
Walker, R. (D)
Wallace, F. R. (D)
Wearn, M. (D)

Bedford
Abbey, G. H. J. (D)
Abele, V. (Cs)
Adams, R. (D)
Adcock, P. (Depot Cont)
Allison, S. (D)
Ambrose, B. (D)
Arnold, H. C. (C)
Ashwell, H. (D)
Austin, T.
Auty, B. (D)
Ball, C. H. (C)
Ball, D. (Cs)
Barboo, B.
Barker, H. M. (Cs)
Barnwell, N. (F)
Bartrum, J. G. (D)
Bass, J. (CHE)
Batchelor, A. S. (Cs)
Battle, D. (SF)

Beavers, M. (Cs)
Beevers, M. S. (Cs)
Bellinger, G. S. (C)
Benney, C. (App F)
Berridge, H. G. (D)
Bidwell, L. J. (CC)
Birkett, M. (D)
Blyth, P. (El)
Bowditch, E. (D)
Bower, I.
Bower, K. (App F)
Bowers, M. (El)
Bradshaw, F. E. H (D)
Brandwood, J. (SF)
Brewer, G. (D)
Brewer, K. R. C. (D)
Brimley, P. (SBB)
Brimley, R. (C)
Brooks, R. L. (D)
Broughton, J. (Asst Area TS, South)
Brown, D. J. (D)
Brown, J. W. (C)
Brown, P. (D)
Buckley, M. (C)
Burgoyne, D. R. (D)
Burley, J. (Vehicle Allocator)
Burley, L. C. (D)
Burnage, R. (C)
Burton, S. (I)

Buvac, D. (F)
Buxton, J. A. (D)
Campbell, F. A. (D)
Carding, P. L. W. (F)
Cassidy, W. A.
Catcheside, C. (D)
Chaplin, A. T. (C)
Chapman, H. G. W. (D)
Ciow, W. J (D)
Clark, S. W. (D)
Cleavey, I. R. (C)
Clough, J. O. (D)
Colby, D. W. (D)
Coleman, R. (C)
Coles, D. (I)
Coles, F. T. (C)
Cook, G. W. (C)
Cooper, J. I. (F)
Corbett
Cornwell, E. (WC)
Course, J. (C)
Cowans, J. (D)
Cox, W. H. (C)
Crawley, P. M. (Cs)
Crook, J. (TSh)
Crouch, E. L. (Cs)
Davies, S.
Dawes, S.
Dawson, H. F. (D)
Day, P. H. (D)

Deans, T. (D)
Denton, L. G. (C)
Diemer, G. L. (C)
Dodson, H. H. (VC)
Donelan, J. J. (C)
Doughty, B. (D)
Duguid, J. A. (D)
Dunn, P. V. (D)
Edwards, R. M. (C)
Ellison, W. (Cricketer)
Elphee, D. (DS)
Etheridge, V. (Cricketer)
Etherington, L. (TSh)
Everett, J. W. (C)
Farr, P. A. (D)
Field, A. (Cl)
Field, R. G. (C)
Fields, A.
Fields, R. (C)
Flute, B. (F)
Foggarty, D.
Ford, A. (I)
Foster, L. (D)
Fowler, E. (El)
France, R. A. (C)
Frost, L. (D)
Frost, R. P. (D)
Garner, R.
Gash, A. E. (D)
Gates, P. (TSh)
Gilby, F. C. (D)
Gilks, R.
Gladwin, E. J. S. (D)
Gleed, M. (St)
Golding, R. G. (D)
Goldstraw, K. (Mechanical
Supervisor)
Goodge, S. H. (D)
Goodwin, S. F. (D)
Goward, G. T. (C)
Grady, W. R. (C)
Graelish, M. (Cs)
Grant, R.
Green, S. V. (D)
Gregg, S. H. (D)
Griffiths, I. (C)
Gumble, M. (Cs)
Hackett, H. G. (D)
Haggerwood, J. (C)
Hakin, J. (D)
Halkett, L. W. (Cs)
Hall, R. B. (D)
Hall, T. (D)
Halliday, A. R. (C)
Halliday, R. (D)
Hammond, A. J. (C)
Handscombe, C.
Hansted, J. E. H. (D)
Harman, R. H. R. (D)
Harris, B. (Cs)
Harris, D. (Schedules &
Development Officer)
Hartley
Hassey, V.
Haynes, P. (TSh)

Haywood, P. A. (C)
Heale, M. (D)
Heaney, M. M. (Cs)
Heathcote, J. (D)
Henderson, C. (DE)
Hill, C. (D)
Hill, D. W. (D)
Hill, M. (P)
Hillier, G. (CHE)
Hinds, K.
Hobbs, L.
Holden, A. (D)
Holmes, C. W. J (D)
Holmes, J. (Garage)
Houghton, A. H. (D)
Howe, E. E (D)
Howes, P. R. (C)
Howes, T. (S)
Hucknall, H. (I)
Hucknall, J. (D)
Hughes, J. (D)
Humphreys, E. E. (D)
Ignjatijevic, M. (SBB)
Ingram, G. (D)
Inskip, E. A. (D)
Irwin, T. (F)
Jackson, C. (D)
Jackson, J. (D)
Jackson, K. V. (D)
Jackson, V. (El)
Jackson, W. E. (D)
Jackson, W. H. (D)
Jacob, G. (C)
Jeapes, J. P. (D)
Jeapes, R. I. (Cs)
Jeavons, W. G. (C)
Jeeps, J. (El)
Jeeves, R. J. (BM)
Jennison, Te (C)
Jewitt, M (TS)
Jiggle, E. F. (DC)
Johnson, F. G. (D)
Johnson, G. (D)
Johnson, M. C. (Cs)
Jones, E. W. (D)
Jones, F. (I)
Jones, F. H. (C)
Joyce, A. (D)
Joyce, E. A. (D)
Juffs, W. F. S. (D)
Kalicanin, D. (Cl)
Kaura, S. (D)
Keech, J. W. (D)
Kester, N. (El)
Kidder, L. A.
King, F. E. (C)
King, I. (Canteen)
Kingstone, I. (SBB)
Kirtley, H. (DI)
Knight, T. (Chargehand
Vehicle I)
Lack, M. C. (D)
Lawrence, W. F. (D)
Layton, J. M. O. (Cs)
Leach, J. (D)

Leadbetter, A. (D)
Leadbetter, J. L. (El)
Leathersich, H. J. (D)
Leeder, P. F. (C)
Leydon, J. (C)
Lloyd, F. L. (Cs)
Logan, B. (Cs)
Lord, G. W. (C)
Lorrimer-George, P.
(Cricketer)
Lovell, R. (D)
Lovett, S.
Luetchford, D. (Dock
Chargehand)
Lunness, T. (I)
Lyall, J. M. (Cs)
Lyons, D. (S)
McCabe, H. B. (C)
McCall, B. (District
Manager, North Beds)
McCally, F. G. (Cs)
McDonald, B. (D)
MacDonald, R. W. (Stores
Van Driver)
McGowan, E. (Cs)
Mahami, H.
Mahon, W. E. (C)
Manchett, O. (Cs)
Manchett, R. W. (D)
Maskell, W. O. (D)
Maxey, S. (D)
May, B. (D)
Mayston, C. W. (D)
Meadows, D. E. (D)
Mechan, F. (D)
Miller, A. R. (I)
Minney, A. R. (D)
Moore, D. H. (D)
Moore, F. (D)
Moore, J. (TSh)
Moule, R. P. (D, Cl)
Mulchinock, R. (C)
Munns, F. W. (C)
Nason, G. (E)
Neal, D. (S)
Nemadic
Nesbit, J. (D)
O'Sullivan, D. (C)
Orral, H. (D)
Page, B. (Cricketer)
Paget, Z. O. (OM)
Parish, A (D)
Payne, K. W. J. (D)
Peacock, H. N. (C)
Peck, A. W. (C)
Perceval, C. (TSh)
Peters, L. L. (C)
Pulley, H. (D)
Rai, B. (D)
Rayner, P.
Reilley, B.
Richards, H. J. (C)
Roberts, G. W (C)
Rothwell, C. A. (C)
Rubery

Rudkin, F. J. (D)
Scholes, R.
Scott, B.
Scott, R. (D)
Sgryoliew, M.
Sharpe, W. L. (F)
Shaw, B. (C)
Shaw, C. (D)
Sheehy, W. (C)
Sheffield, C. W.
Shelton, C. R. (D)
Shelton, C. R. (D)
Shopland, E. C. (D)
Shopland, E. J. (D)
Short, G. (D)
Shuttleworth, A. (E)
Singh, B.
Singh, S. (D)
Smith, A. B. C. (C)
Smith, B. (D)
Smith, E. M. (Cs)
Smith, K. G. (D)
Smith, R. (Skilled Coach
Repairer)
Sorrell, E. C. (D)
Southam, H. C. (D)
Spray, R. R. W. (S)
Spurgeon, C. A. (C)
Stafford, K. (I)
Stanley, R. H. (D)
Stewart, L. (C)
Stokes, A. (D)
Stokes, J. E. (Cs)
Stokes, R. (D)
Strangeway, R. (E Manager)
Stroud, F. A. (D)
Swain, H. (D)
Sye, B. (Depot TM)
Tembey, R. (F)
Thompson, G. H. (D)
Thompson, H. J. (D)
Thompson, J. W. (D)
Thorman, C. F. (C)
Thurlow, P. (E, South)
Tolson, E. (Cs)
Turner, A. A. (D)
Turner, E. (D)
Tyler, J. (TSh Manager)
Valentine, K. M.
Wade, J. (D)
Wain, D. (Cricketer)
Walker, A. (D)
Walsh, J. J. (C)
Ward, D. (D)
Ward, P. (D)
Ware, W. E. (D)
Warnes, H. W. (C)
Watson, D. J. (D)
Watson, E. R. (I, Output
Foreman)
Watson, J. (Cs)
Watson, J. O. (D)
Watson, N. (TSh)
Watt, T. J. (D)
Watts, J. L. (F)

West, J. (TSh)
Whiffin, J. W. (C)
Whitmore, R. B. (I)
Wilkins, E. V. (C)
Williams, D. (T)
Willis, D. V. G. (C)
Wolfe, P. M. (Cs)
Wood, H. (D, photographer)
Woodruff, T. (St)
Woods, A. (D)
Woods, P. M. (Ck)
Woolston, J. (Skilled Body-fitter)
Worboys, L. (D)
Wright, E. D. (Csr)
York (C)
Young, A. C. (C)
Yourin, M.

Biggleswade
Albone, R. (D, FC)
Ambrose, B. (D)
Anderson, A. C. (D)
Arnold, M. (D, ex-Birch Bros)
Askew, S. (Office Sec)
Askham, A. F. (D)
Auburn, T. (D)
Battson, J. (F)
Beagley, F. (D, Service)
Birley, S.
Booth
Bradburn, M. (D)
Broggi, T. (D)
Brown, H. (F in Charge)
Brown, N. (E)
Bull, S. (D)
Burton, J.
Campion, F. (D)
Chambers, R. (D)
Chenery, B. (D)
Clutton, E. (Cs)
Cole, B. (Cs)
Cook, E. (Cl)
Crawley, S. (D)
Dashwood, G. (I)
Dent, S. R. (D)
Desborough, D. (Sec)
Dixon, C. (D)
Duggan, G. (C)
Elt, J. (D)
Endersby, M. (D)
Finding, F. (D)
Finding, R. (D)
Fountain, B. (D)
Gamble, F. (Cl)
Gatehouse, F.
Giddings, G. (D)
Gilbert, P. E. (D)
Godfrey, I. (D)
Gravestock, W. H. (D)
Gray, H.
Gudgin, B. (D)
Hall, M. (D)
Hallybone, D. (D)

Hann, D. (D)
Hart, L. R. (C)
Hazel, J. (D)
Henderson, K. (F)
Hibbert, W. (D)
Hill, G. (D)
Holby (I)
Hope, T.
Houghton, M. (D)
Housden, M. B. (Cs)
Izzard, B. (F)
Jeeves
Jones, S. (D)
Jones, V. (Cs)
Merry, D. (S)
Moor, D. (D)
Norris, R. (C)
Offin, T. (D)
Palastonja, L. (D)
Parker, V. E. (Cs)
Pates, R. A. (C)
Payne, A. (D)
Pepper, G. (C)
Phillips, B. (D)
Phillips, R. (D)
Price, H. (D)
Rayner, P. (D)
Reters, R. (D)
Robertson, J. (D)
Robinson, R. (C)
Rook, F. A. (C)
Sabey, P. (D)
Scholes, R. (D)
Scott, R. (Cl)
Smith, C. Y. (S)
Smith, G. (C)
Smith, M. (D)
Spinks, J.
Stafford, C. (E)
Standerline, D. J. (D)
Theobald, G. (MF)
Tyler, C. (F)
Tyson, J. (D)
Ward, V.
Warland, I. (D)
Whitemore, R.
Whitfield, F. (D)
Wildgoose, G. (D)
Wilkins, G. (D)
Wilkins, K. (Cs)
Wilkinson, P. (D)
Williams, F. (D)
Williams, T. (D)
Worboys, L. (D)

Bletchley
Bishop, J. (D)
Bootle, J. (I)
Broderick, P. R. (D)
Carter (Cs)
Chilton, H. (first female I)
Chown, L. (D)
Coley, D. (D)
Coughlan, M. (D)
Crockett, F. (D, Union rep)

Davies, H. H. (C)
Fisk, T. (D)
Gornel, C. (C)
Harding, D. (D)
Joyce, S. (C)
Lambert, A. (I in Charge)
Mackenzie, D. C. S. (D)
Masters, P. (D, I)
Morgan, L. (Cs)
New, P. (D)
Oakes (D, I)
Phillips, B. (D)
Tuffen, A. (Cs)
White, C. (D)
Whyte, J. (D)
Wood, D. (Area TS, West)
Young, D. (D)

Brackley
Batey, J. (TSh Manageress)
Cummings, H. (TSh)
Dalton, D. (TSh)
Rice, S. (TSh)
Woods, S. (TSh)

Corby
Bird, R. (I)
Britten, A. (D)
Burns, J.
Calland, R. (D)
Davies, J. I. (F)
Dickens, C. (D)
Djukic, O. B.
Drew, J. O. (Assistant OM)
Evans, S. (D)
Fennel, L. E.
Fisher, J. (D)
Fitzsimmons, D. (D)
Ford, L. (DC)
Ford, S. L. (Revenue Control)
Godsell, M. (D)
Grantham, S. (D)
Hearn, M. (Revenue Protection I)
Hopkins, R. (C)
Hudson, K. (D)
James, N. (D)
Jones, M. (Depot TM)
Kerr, H. (Relief Cont)
King, G. O (Chargehand F)
Knox, R. (D)
Langley, D. (D)
Lawson, W. (D)
McBlaine, D. U.
McEleney, C. (I)
McGilway, P. F. (D)
Miller, M. (D)
Mitchell, P. (D)
Nicholson, M. (Enquiry Ck)
Osborne, G. (D)
Polek, S. (D)
Pollock, S (D)
Potts, J. (D)
Quayle, S. (D)

Reid, P.
Rice, B. (D)
Robinson, D. (D)
Robinson, N. (D)
Sangster, A. Snr (D)
Simpson, C. (D)
Singh, K. (D)
Smith, A.
Swainster, M. (Booking Office Ck)
Swanston, M. A. (CC)
Taylor, J. E. (D)
Tilley, B. (D)
Woolacott, G. (Maintenance)

Daventry
Smith, P. R. (I)

Desborough
Bell, R. (D)
Feazey, B.
Freestone, J. E. (D)
Gilman, D. J. (D)
Holmes, W. (D, Union Branch Chairman)
Hunt, R.
Page, A. W. (C)
Panter, H. W.
Smith, A. (D)
Springthorpe, M. (D)
Starkey, B. F. (D)
Starkey, S. A. (D)
Taylor, L. J. (D)
Willis, E. M.

Dunstable
Pullen, C. (Enquiry kiosk)

Hitchin
Barnsley, H. (I)
Benson, M. (D)
Brown, R. (D)
Burd, S. J. (S)
Byatt, S. (D)
Chalkley, G. (D)
Chalkley, P. (D)
Draper, D. (D, Cl)
Duncan, J. (D)
Edwards, D. (F)
Gaffney, R. (D)
Hatch, B. (D)
Holby, A. (D)
Holby, D. Jnr (D)
Holby, D. Snr (I)
Holloway, K. (D)
Kenyon, B. (S)
Knight, S. (D)
Morrison, M. (Cs)
Moulton, R. (D)
Osborne, R. (D)
Pateman, J. (DE)
Pollicarpo, J. (D)
Puttick, J. (D)
Reeves, I. (D)

Robinson, A. R. (D)
Saggers, J. (D)
Scribenger, G. (D)
Spicer, C. N. (F)
Spicer, L. (D)
Swain, C. (Service Man)
Vincent, J. G. (C)
Walton, B.
Watson, V. A. (C)
Welstead, J. (D)
Wye, S. (D)

Huntingdon
Beal, A. J. (D)
Bradbury, T. (D)
Burnside, G. (D)
Burr, R. (D)
Carley, I. (D)
Cooper, J. (I)
Crawford, K. (D)
Darline, T. (D)
Darlow, J. (MF)
Foulds (D)
Francis, D.
Gibson, S. W. (D)
Griffiths, P. (DE)
Gummer, L. (D)
Hannibal, R. (D)
Heath, V. (Cont)
Hehir, J. (DM)
Hehir, P. (Office)
Hinds, B. (I in Charge)
Hodgin (D)
Karley, M. (D)
Lane, A. (C)
Lawrence, P. (D)
Leach, D. (F)
Leach, M. (F)
McMordie, M. (Cs)
McMordie, W. (D)
Malik, Z.
Mead, G. (S)
Mead, T. (DM)
Musk, E. (D)
Nicholetti (D)
Perry, R. (C)
Phillips, S. T. (DI)
Phrimpton, D. (D)
Reedman, S.
Simmons, A. (D)
Smith, B. (D)
Smith, P. (E)
Spicer (I in Charge)
Szurhaluk, B. (F)
Tiller, S. H. (C)
Verrall, J. (D)
Watson, D. (D)
West (D)
Wheeler, J. (Cs)
Wheeler, T. (D)
Wilson, R. (Cl)

Irthlingborough
Craddock, J. (BM)
Gibbs, A. L. (BM)

Griffin, A. L. (BM)
Tyler, R. (BM)

Kettering
Adams, D. C.
Adams, F. (D)
Alderman, A. O.
Alfano, A. C.
Allen, A. T.
Allen, C.
Allen, D. A. (C)
Allen, J. T.
Allen, R.
Allsopp, A.
Allsopp, M. (Cs)
Amin, V. M. (C)
Anderson, J.
Andrews, E. (D)
Annets, J. E.
Arnold, R.
Ashby, J. P.
Ashelford, J. W. (D)
Attrill, M.
Ayres, N.
Bailey, J. C. (D)
Bains, H. S.
Baker, B. J. H.
Baker, D.
Barker, C. A.
Barker, F. M.
Barker, P.
Barrie, A.
Barrie, G.
Barton, B. R. (D, DI)
Barton, R. M. (D)
Barwell
Bates, S. H. (D)
Batten, H. (Ck)
Bayes, L. A. (D)
Baynes, M.
Beasley, P. J.
Beeston, B. (DI)
Bence, J. (D)
Bennett, C.
Bhambra, J. S.
Bialek, P. (D)
Blackwell, A. A.
Blissett, E.
Blissett, M.
Boyle, J.
Brace, N. J (Output)
Branson, S. R.
Bray, F. (C)
Bray, S. D. (D)
Brennan, A. V.
Brian, E.
Buckby, R.
Buettner, M. H.
Bulley, H. V. (Lorry Driver)
Bulpit, L.
Burford, I. (D)
Burgin, G.
Burnage, B.
Burnes, D.
Burrows, E. G.

Burton, R. H.
Byfield, P. G. (D)
Campbell, A.
Carr, G.
Carrington, C. (I)
Carter, R.
Carter, S. G.
Cartwright, S.
Carvell, M.
Cassidy, J.
Catalano, G. (F)
Cave, M. (D)
Chambers, K. (D)
Chambers, S.
Chenery, G. O. (D)
Cherry, D. (I)
Chessman, W. T.
Clark, D. A.
Clark, D. W.
Clarke, R. (D)
Clarke, R. I. (D)
Clarke, V.
Clarke, W. (WC)
Clay, E. (Canteen)
Clements, W.
Clipston, F. A.
Clipstone, H. J. (D)
Coates, G. (D)
Coe, G. (Ck)
Coker, B.
Cole, B. W.
Coleman, R. W.
Collins, R.
Constable, E.
Conway, W. (D)
Cook, F. R.
Cooper, H. A. (C)
Cooper, L. (D)
Cooper, R.
Copeland, B. F.
Corbin, J. (D)
Core, M. (D)
Cormack, J. (D)
Cornwall, P. W. (C)
Cotton, A.
Cotton, G. K. (D)
Coulson, M. (Canteen)
Cowe, M. (D)
Cowen, J.
Cox, S. A. (C)
Coyle, A. M.
Craswell, S. J.
Craxford, A.
Crumpton, D.
Curtis, R.
Davies, B.
Davis, G. K. (F)
Dawkes, T.
Docherty, C.
Dodds, M. (D)
Douglas, M.
Drage, P. (D)
Draper, M. E (CHF)
Driver, C.

Driver, L. G. (D)
Driver, S. B.
Dunkley, W. C. E. (D)
Dwyer, N.
Eaton, A.
Edgson, T. (D)
Egan, N. (D)
Elmore, D. (App)
Essam, S. G. (D)
Evans, M. (BB)
Falkner, A.
Farrelly, P. (D)
Feakin, A. (D)
Fenton, R. A. (Booking Ck)
Fett, P.
Fisher, S.
Forsyth, M. (D)
Forsyth, N. (D)
Foster, G. R. (D)
Fox, D. I. (D)
Fox, J.
Frankham, V. (D)
Fraser, D. J.
Freeman, W. C.
Frost, T.
Frost, W. E.
Fuller, D.
Gardner, D. W. (D)
Gardner, M. C. (WC)
Gardner, W. J. (C)
Gartshore, E.
Gentle, L. (TS)
Giddings, S.
Glazewski, T. (D)
Gloynn, K.
Gobbett, D. (D)
Goodman, G. (D)
Goodman, S. L.
Goodway, T.
Gordon, E.
Gore, W. G. J.
Graham, A.
Graham, R. B.
Grantham, A. (D)
Green, K. (D)
Green, R. (BB)
Groves, J.
Guerin, J. A. (D)
Guest, A. L. M.
Hadden, B. (OM)
Hadden, R. (D)
Halliwell, S.
Halser, T. O. (C)
Hampson, C. F.
Hampson, C. H.
Hampson, J.
Hanagan, D.
Hanger, A. (D)
Hannah, T.
Harper, E.
Harvey, G. (D)
Haycocks, P. A.
Hayland, C.
Headlands, E. H. (D)

Heath, L. (D)
Hegn, B. (Ck)
Hendry, M. (Cl)
Hilliard, J. R. (D)
Hillier, A. J.
Hodges, P.
Hogan, P. (SF)
Hogan, R. A. (Enquiry Ck)
Hogarth, P. (D)
Hollis, J. (D)
Holmes, H.
Holmes, S. (D)
Hooton, F. (DI)
Horsley, K. M.
Hughes, M. (D)
Humpreys, D. H. (D)
Incles, G. A. (D)
Ingram, F. R. (I)
Irons, A. J.
Irons, H. H. (D)
Irons, J. E.
Irons, P. D.
Italiano, A. (F)
Jackson, C.
James, D. G. (D)
James, L.
James, R. G.
Jarman, L.
Jeffs, K. R.
Jocinder
Jones, A.
Jones, A. N.
Jones, R. (D)
Joyce, J. A.
Jubb, G. (D)
Keen, A.
Key, A. R.
Key, R. H.
Kiche, A. D.
King, H. E (Cl)
King, J.
King, P. W.
King, S.
Kinslow, C.
Kirby, J. G.
Klemis, M. D.
Knowles, D.
Konarczak, T. (D)
Kumar, V.
Kyle, J.
Lanza, B.
Lavender, P.
Laywood, B. C. (D)
Leach, A.
Lee, A.
Lee, B. (D)
Lee, R. H.
Lees, S.
Lemay, S.
Leton, J. A.
Lettin, C. (D)
Linnett, K.
Litchfield, P. S.
Logan, F.
Long, D.

Long, M. (D)
Lumsden, A. (Cl)
Lynn, D.
Mabbutt, H.
McAlwane, G. (D)
McBean, K.
McCammon, A. G. (Cl)
McFadden, M.
McGeorge, M. (D)
McHulay, J.
McKenna, M. E. (Cs)
McRay, M.
McTaggart, A.
Maddison, S. J.
Main, J.
Malcolm, L.
Mansfield, A.
March, D. J. (D)
Marriott, G. (St)
Marsh, L. A. (D, Mayor of
Kettering)
Maslin, D. E. (D)
Matlock, B. (D)
Maxwell
May, V.
Mayhew, S. L. (C)
Meecham, J.
Melia, E. (D)
Mellen, G. H. (D)
Mellors, B. S.
Merrill, C. M.
Millar, B.
Minney, V.
Mistri, J. (D)
Moisey, F. E. (D)
Moisey, J. H.
Monk, B.
Moore, F. (D, ex-Welford)
Morran, R. H.
Morrison, C.
Munday, L.
Murdin, A. (D)
Murray, H. (Cl)
Murray, W.
Muscutt, R. (Building
Maintenance E)
Mustin, P. A. (D)
Mutton, L. A.
Naylor, K.
Needle, G.
Newlyn, L.
Newman, B. F.
Newton, D.
Nix, F. J. (D)
Nix, J. W. (D)
Noon, D. J. (I)
Northern, A. G.
Northover, S.
O'Rourke, J. (D)
Odams, A. G (D)
Ogden, A. S. (Union
official/Cont)
Ogilvie, M. A. (Csr)
Oram, T. J. (D)
Owen, A. T.

Pack, F. W. (D)
Palmer, W.
Pamplin, D. (C)
Panter, H. S. (C)
Panter, W. A.
Patrick, J. (D)
Paul, J.
Payne, D.
Peacock, J.
Pell, W.
Penny, R.
Pethers, D. A.
Pettit, H. C. (C)
Pike, A. N (Asst Manager)
Pipe, A.
Pipe, B. R.
Pitt, F. R. (C)
Porch, C.
Porteous, J. (F)
Preston, J. W. (D)
Priestley, G.
Pullen, A. R.
Pullen, R.
Quayle, C. (D)
Ramsey, R. (DS)
Rawabany, K. G.
Read, R.
Read, R. W.
Redhead, R.
Redken, B. A.
Redley, S. A. (C)
Reed, B.
Reed, C. (D)
Reed, E. L. (National
Express hostess)
Reed, R.
Remmer, S.
Rendley, M.
Rhoades, B.
Rice, P. B.
Rice, R. F.
Richardson, M.
Roberts, T. (Ck, D)
Roche, O. (D)
Ross, D. L.
Routh, A.
Rowney, G. (El)
Rowney, M.
Rowney, P. F. (C)
Rowney, R. (Cs)
Rutter, A. (D)
Ruxton, G. A.
Saddington, D. B.
Sallis, R. (C)
Sangster, M. (Canteen)
Saunders, K. (D)
Savage, C.
Schnidt, K.
Scott, A.
Seymour, L.
Seymour, M.
Shandley, D.
Sharma, M.
Sharpe, D.
Shepherd, G.

Shipton, N. (D)
Sims, C. (I)
Sinclair, D. (F)
Singh, D. M. (D)
Singh, G.
Singh, H. (D)
Singh, P.
Sirrell, R.
Slater, A. W. (D)
Smallman, R.
Smith, B.
Smith, B. Snr (D)
Smith, C. (Chief Csr)
Smith, C. E. (I)
Smith, C. Y. (I)
Smith, D. T. B.
Smith, E.
Smith, G. A. (D)
Smith, J. G. (D)
Smith, K.
Smith, L.
Smith, P. P.
Smith, R. A. (D, I)
Smith, R. P.
Smith, R. S
Smith, T. M. (D)
Smith, W. (DM)
Spence, N. L.
Spencer, K. G.
Spolton, D. E.
Stanion, G. A.
Stanley, H. T. (F)
Stapleton, E. A. (D)
Starkey, S. (D)
Stefaniak, W.
Stevens, E. (Sec)
Stevens, H.
Stevenson, W.
Stolarski, L. (D)
Stone, M.
Strickland, T. (D)
Stronner, M. J.
Summers, D.
Sutherland, H. T. (D)
Swann, A. L. (VC)
Swannell, S. (D)
Swerkle, M.
Tartaglia, T. (D)
Taseland, J. K.
Taylor, J. E. (D; killed at
work)
Tegg, S.
Thamar, M. A.
Thomas, I. N.
Thompson, B. (D)
Thurlow, J. S.
Thursby, E. (Cs)
Timms, F.
Tinsley, A. (D)
Tobierre, J.
Toms, D. (D)
Towerton, S. I.
Townsend, T. (DE)
Transfard
Turner, R. A. (D)

Turpin, M.
Tuson, M.
Vakkachen, B.
Van Beck, D. (D)
Vengalil, J.
Viliers, D. (F)
Vincent, E. W. (D)
Walker, E. R. (Sec)
Walker, G. H.
Wall, C. (D)
Wallace, D.
Waller, G. T.
Walsh, P.
Ward, K.
Wardley, D. (D)
Warren, B. (D)
Warwick, F. (D)
Watson, N.
Watson, P. W.
Webb, J. (D)
Webb, V. G. (D)
Wells, A.
Wells, B.
Wells, D. N. (D)
Wesley, R.
West, J. H.
Westley, H. J. (D)
Weston, C.
White, A. W.
White, B. (D)
White, F. L. (Labourer)
White, J.
White, R. (D)
White, S.
White, W. R.
Whitney, D.
Whyte, J. R.
Wilby, W. D.
Willis, K.
Wills, J. E. (I)
Wilson, M.
Wilson, R. (D)
Wilson, W.
Wittering, T. (Union Branch Secretary)
Wood, W. J.
Woodward, R.
Wuiphs, L.
York, G. D. (Chargehand)
Yorkston, R. C. (D)
Young, T.

Leighton Buzzard
Couchman, T. (D)
Dimmock, F. (D, C)
Donaldson, G. (D)
Gall, R. W. (C)
Hammond, B. (C)
Harris, R. G.
Heffer, J. (D)
Horselor, D. (D)
Horwood, J. (D)
Kingham, H. (D)
McDonald, V. (Cs)
McTeer, N. (D)

Morgan, F. H. (D)
Oliver, M. (Cs)
Sear, W. G.
Shipley, J. (D)
Stone, R. O. G. (D)
Stone, R. O. Y. (D)
Tierney, P. D. (Cs)
Tucker, A. P. J. (D)
Tucker, P. J. (D)
Turney, D. (Cs)
Turney, J. (I)

Luton
Anderson, A. (D)
Anderson, K. (D)
Ashworth, J. (Footballer)
Auburn, D. L.
Baker, M. (D)
Barnard, B. (Ck)
Barnard, R. W (Output Foreman)
Bartlett, D. (D)
Bass, L. R.
Bates, W. H. (D)
Battersby, D. (D)
Blackburne, T. (D)
Blake, L. (D)
Blessing, M. (App)
Boston, S. (D, Footballer)
Bowland, M. (D)
Brady, K. (C)
Brahim, I. (F)
Braidwood, J. (I)
Bright, L.
Brightman, D. (MF)
Brown, 'Captain' K. M. E (Vehicle radiator filler)
Brown, D. (F)
Browne, A. (D)
Browne, G. W. L. (D)
Bunyan, I. (Cl)
Burton, I. (D)
Butler, P. (Cl)
Butler, W. (Cs)
Bywaters (F)
Carrington, R. (Footballer)
Catt, B. (D)
Catt, W. A.
Chance, I. (F)
Chapman
Clark, C. O.
Clark, H. K. (D)
Clarke, G. (F)
Clarke, M. (D)
Coates (Ck)
Cooper, N. J.
Coughlan (D)
Craig, S. (Body Shop Chargehand)
Cubbins, T. (D)
Dale, J. (F)
Davis, A. E. (D)
Dearman, G. (D)
Denison, P. (F)
Derring, M.

Donohue, M. (Cs)
Dunne, J. (Footballer)
Edmonds, G. (I)
Ellis, C. (F)
Emery, R. (D)
Everleigh, K. (I)
Farrell, A. (D)
Fennah, J. (PA)
Fields, M. (Cs)
Fitt, C.
Forde, B. (D)
Fowlcr, M. (Body Shop)
Frazer (F)
Freeley, K. (D)
Frith, R. (D)
Gallagher, R. (C)
Garlick, A. (Cl)
Garlick, R. (D, Director of Luton & District)
Gatehouse, F. (Mechanical Supervisor)
Goldsmith, H. G.
Goodison, D. (Asst E)
Goodyear, K. (D)
Goss, D. (D)
Grace, L. (C, Special Duties)
Grafton, P. (D)
Gregory, S. (D)
Haggerty, R. A. (F)
Hanaman, J.
Harrison (Ck)
Hawkins, G. (Chief Traffic Asst/Super)
Haydon, C.
Higgins, R. (S)
Hill, A. (D)
Hoare, E. (Cs)
Hodges, W. (Shift F)
Honeywood, G. (D)
Howes, A. (D)
Hubbocks, M. (D)
Hughes, E. (D)
Hughes, J. (D)
Hunt, S. (Footballer)
Iannett, J. (Cl)
Jones, B. (Footballer)
Jones, D. (D)
Jones, R.
Joseph, P. (D)
Karley, M. (D)
Kellegher, J. (D)
Kendrick, B. (C)
Kendrick, W. T. (C)
Kilidas (F)
Kilpatrick, C. (D)
King, A. (D)
King, J. (CC)
Kostars, E. (D)
Kostorz, T. (D)
Lake, A. (D, footballer)
Laney, K.
Leonard, P. (D, Driver Trainer)
Lewington, A. (Footballer)

Lovegrove, F. (D)
McCagh, J. (App)
McCann, A. (Chief Wages Ck)
McEnaney, P. (D)
Macey, M. (D)
McGovern, M. J. (D)
McGovern, P.
McKarr, T. (Footballer)
Mackey (F)
McMullen, M. (D)
McNiffe, J. (D, FC)
McPhee, A. (Private Hire Ck)
Major, M. (Footballer)
Manning, L. (Shunter)
Mapp, B. (Footballer)
Mapp, M. (Footballer)
Maris, J. (DS)
Martin, P.
Martin, R. (D)
Mastrogiovanni, G. (Footballer)
Mead, B. (Footballer)
Meek, B. A. (Charting)
Miles, E. R. (D, Union Branch Chairman)
Mitchell, G. (D)
Mitchell, N. (D)
Morgan, J. (Running Shift Foreman)
Mortimer, B. (Footballer)
Mountain, J. (D)
Mulford, R. (Footballer)
Mulligan, D. (I)
Munn, R. (D)
Murtagh, E. (Night watchman)
Nabarro, P. (D)
Newman, E. (Reception/Telephonist)
Newman, G. (Foreman)
O'Brien, A. (Admin Officer)
O'Brien, J. (I)
O'Connor, N. (Cs)
O'Dell, W.
O'Donnell, W. (SF)
O'Kane, R.
O'Neill, D. (Footballer)
Orr, M. (Cl)
Pancholi (D)
Pepper, S. T.
Pitcher, C. (D)
Poett, C. (Cl)
Powell, P. (D)
Price, I. (Cl)
Price, W. (D, Driver of the Year competitor)
Priestley, D. (D)
Rashid (D)
Reading, D. (D)
Roberts, C. (Asst DS)
Robinson, K.
Rogers, M. (D)
Rolfe, C. (I)

Rolfe, H. R. (I)
Rose, A. (D, I)
Rose, C. (Ck)
Row, F. (D)
Rumbold, R. (S)
Rutter, C. (D)
Saddington, T. (F)
Sales, R. (D)
Searle, B. (D)
Shelford, K. (D)
Shelley, A. (I)
Smith, C. W. J. T. (D)
Smith, E. (Area E)
Smith, J. (Cs)
Spacey, M. (D)
Spary, F. (D)
Spary, R. (D)
Spooner, M. (Footballer)
Steward, R. M. (Cs)
Steward, V. (Cs)
Stewart, D. (D)
Stewart, P. (Footballer)
Swann, B. (D)
Taylor, D. (Footballer)
Taylor, M. (D)
Thrussel, C. (Typist/
Telephonist)
Travidi, J. (D)
Trodden, M. (DE)
Upton, D. (Director)
Upton, L. G. (Body Shop
Chargehand)
Usami, M. (D)
Uttley, E. (Garage)
Verrall, J. (D)
Wakefield, R. (D)
Wakelin, N. (D)
Walker (F)
Wall, T. (Footballer)
Waters, G. (D)
Waters, J. (D)
Watersfield, T. (D)
Watts, J. (C, crew D, OPO
D)
Watts, T. J.
Webb, R. (El)
Wells, R.
White, A. (I)
White, B. (District Manager,
South Beds)
White, J. (D)
Whitton, J. (Area E, South)
Wilcox (D)
Wilderspin, R. L. F.
Wilson, J. (D)
Wilson, S. (Cl)
Wood, J. (C)
Wood, K. (Footballer)
Wood, P.

Milton Keynes
Bailey, B. (I)
Barraclough, B. (DE)
Booker, P. (Schedules &
Development Officer)

Bowen, K. (D)
Burgess, S. (TSh)
Coughlan, M. (D)
Craswell, J. (D)
Craswell, S. (D)
Cross, L. (C)
Duffy, M. (D)
Fell, G. (App)
Freiss, S. (D)
Gibbons, D. (Traffic Office)
Goodman, S. U. (Officer)
Haynes, B. O. (Service Man)
King, I. (DC)
Lambert, A. W. H (CC, I)
Lavender, L. (TSh)
Mackrill, K. (Map
Supervisor)
Mason, A. (DAB D)
McAllister, I. (Area TS,
North)
Potter, T. (Shunter)
Prydderch, B. (Office)
Reader, N. (C)
Robinson, P. (Supervisor)
Rowell, G. (DE)
Savile, J. (D)
Smith, M. (S)
Smith, N. (Schedules
Officer/Super)
Stewart, I (DAB D/Map
Supervisor)
Ward, A. (DS)
Warner, B. (EM, North)
Whitaker, W. (D)

Northampton
Bazeley, W. A. (D)
Belham, B.
Bell, L.
Berrill, B.
Billingham, M. J. (Asst
Super, North)
Bland, A. (TSh)
Bowden, J. (D)
Bowman, J. (D)
Briggs, C. (F; died in
service)
Briody, T. (C)
Brittain, K. (Running Shift
Foreman)
Britten, D. (D)
Britten, J. (Cs)
Brown, B. O. (D)
Brown, C.
Bull, L. (D)
Bull, R. C. (D)
Burditt, R. (D)
Buswell, B. (D)
Butler, H. (Commercial
Administrator)
Butler, M. A. (OM)
Byron, G. (National Express
Cont)
Bywaters, E. (F)
Carroll, K.

Carter, L.
Causebrook, A. (Admin
Asst)
Chesterfield, K. (D)
Chrisp, M. (D)
Christian, R. (Asst Area TS)
Clack, M.
Clack, P. (D)
Clark, C. (T)
Clipston, H. R. (Ck, D)
Cockerill, W. H. (I)
Colton, A. (Schedules)
Cook, P. (F)
Cooper, E. (Chargehand Cl)
Cox, F. (Depot Chargehand
Cl)
Cox, M. A. (CSO)
Cox, M. J. (D)
Crick, J. (D)
David, K.
Davies, J. I. (D)
Davies, R. (DS)
De Santis, P. (Commercial
Administrator)
Deane, P. (D)
Doovic, P. A.
Doyle, M. (Canteen)
Duffy, F. (D)
Durrant, M. (D)
Dyball, R. (E)
Ellis, E. (Asst Cook, Café)
Ellis, J. F. (D)
Eyres, R. (Cs)
Fairman, J. (D)
Fall, R. F. (Ck)
Farley, C. T. (Cs)
Faulkner, R. E. (D)
Fawcett, A. (Admin Officer)
Fawdon, C. (D)
Fenton, G. (Canteen)
Fincher, W. E.
Flatery, L. (SBB)
Foster, G. (DI)
Freeman, D. (I)
Frost, J. (C)
Frost, L. E.
Fryer, D. (TSh)
Fulman, G. E. (D)
Galvin, R.
Garlick, J. (C)
Gates, T. (EM)
George, R. (D)
Gordon, T. (Depot Csr)
Graham, D.
Griggs, J. (D)
Guy, T. (D)
Hall, H.
Halton, M. (Canteen
Manageress)
Hamilton, J. (T)
Hannant, P. (TSh Ck)
Harrison, F. (I)
Hasler (D)
Haynes, M.
Head, C. (TSh)

Headland, E. H. (D)
Heginbotham, D. (D)
Heginbotham, G. (D)
Henderson, A. (EM)
Heron, R. (D)
Hickerson, D. F. (Ck)
Hillyard, R. (CSO)
Hinds, T. (EM)
Hobbs, J. (DE)
Hogben, A.
Holton, J. W. (C)
Honey, J. (Workshop
Supervisor)
Horne, R. G. (D)
Horner, E. (D)
Horner, G. E. (D)
Horner, G. I. L. (D)
Houghton, A. (D)
Houghton, H. I. C. (C)
Hurnell, M. (Output
Inspector/PT Ck)
Hyde, H. F. (C)
John, A. D. (Uniforms
Dept)
Johnson, F. A. (D)
Johnstone, C. (MSC)
Jones, L. R. (D)
Kehoe, T. (D)
Kelly, M. (D)
Kelly, P. J. (D)
Kemp, R. (F)
Kerr, D. (D)
Kilby, A. (E Sec)
Knight, A. (MSC)
Lack, M. (D)
Lack, W. A. (Cl, D)
Lewis, M. (C)
Lilford, S. G. (C)
Lloyd, R. (C)
Lloyd, R. E. (I)
Lovell, S. (D)
Lowe, J. (C)
Mabbutt, H. (C)
Mace, P. A. (Mechanic)
Mace, R.
Mace, S.
Machin, J. (C)
Mahoney, W.
Mallon, K. (CSO)
Mann, G. (D)
Maycock, N. C. (District
TS)
Meacher, G. (D)
Meek, B. (Csr)
Meredith, W. (C)
Merry, J. (Wages)
Merryfield, W. J. (D)
Mills, B. (D)
Mills, W. J. (D)
Mold, D. (I)
Mortimer, F. C. S. (D)
Mullins, M. (D)
Neal, G. (SF)
Neal, R. (D)
Needle, R. C. (I)

Newman, F. (D)
Nicholson, W. (D)
O'Connor, D (C, TR)
O'Sullivan, F.
Page, D. (Cs)
Palmer, D. (Canteen Manageress)
Palmer, S. (Ck)
Pantling, E. (Cs)
Parker, N. (WC)
Patchsea, P. (D)
Peet, A. (MSC)
Perin, R. (C)
Perrin, R. W. (C)
Perrin, W. (C)
Perryman, C. (D, CSO)
Phillips, J. (Depot Storesperson)
Poulter, T. (DI)
Pratt, S. F. (D)
Putman, G.
Reece, B. (D)
Reeve, H. (D)
Reynolds, A. (TSh)
Russell, P. (D)
Sankey, D. (D)
Savage, B. (D)
Savage, W. C. B. (D)
Sawkins, E. M (Café)
Sharpe, R.
Slinn, D. (Mobile I)
Smart, J. (D)
Smith, L. E. (D)
Smith, L. G. (D)
Smith, R (EM)
Smith, T. (Detailer)
Smith, T. H.
Speachley, N. W. (D)
Stafford, W. (D)
Stevens, A. W. (D)
Stock, E. W. (D)
Stockley, C.
Stolk, A.
Stuart, M. (TSh)
Sweeney, T. (D)
Tacchuo, J.
Teear, B. (D)
Thomas, K (T, TSh)
Todd, H. H.
Todd, R (TSh)
Tomkins, R. (TSh)
Toms, S. (T)
Toms, S. (TSh)
Traynor, N. (MSD)
Treacy, E. (Depot Storesperson)
Turner, D. (D)
Van Hoof, R. (D)
Wakefield, B.
Wakeling, N. (C)
Wakeling, R. (C)
Walton, R. (Union official)
Warren, W. J. (D)
Warwick, J. (Detailer)
Watts, R. O. (D)

Wedgebrow, M. (Running Shift F)
Welford, R. (D)
Wellington, J. (E Supervisor)
Wesley, P. (Van Driver)
West, W. (Asst DM)
Westley, P. (D)
Westley, R. (Mother Christmas)
Westwood, R. (TSh Manager)
Whall, B. (TSh)
White, H. S. (D)
White, W.
Wiggins, N.
Wileman, E. (TSh)
Wileman, L. (TSh)
Williams, R. (D)
Wilton, R. A.
Winforah, S. (Canteen)
Wing, P.
Wood, J. W. G. (C)
Woolmore, P. J. (Area E, West)
Wright, L. (D)
Yeo, L. (TSh)
York, G. E. (D)

Northampton Central Works

Abbott, N. (SBB)
Adams, F. (P)
Adams, P. (Asst E)
Aldesworth, A. (P, Signwriter)
Allen, D. N. (SF)
Allen, S. Y. (P)
Anderson, R.
Arnold, T. (Uniform St)
Ashton, C. (P)
Baker, D.
Bamford, M. (El)
Bass, S. J. (Body Shop)
Bates, A. L.
Bellham, B.
Berry, M. J. (CHF)
Billson, P. (P)
Blackwell, B. (P)
Bliss, P.
Blunt, T. (App F)
Blunt, Y. (UCE)
Bodger, J. (Chairman, UCE)
Brown, B. (Cl)
Brown, H.
Brown, M. (App F)
Brown, N.
Burbidge, D. (P)
Burks, W. (P)
Burt, B. (P)
Care, C. (P)
Carr, M. (Chief E)
Carroll, P.
Cartland, J.
Catlin, L. (P)

Chamberlain, S.
Chambers, B. (P)
Chambers, J. (P)
Chambers, T. (P)
Charleton, J. (F)
Charlton, J.
Childs, M. (Stores Ck)
Clark, R. (P)
Clegg, K. A. (Foreman)
Collins, O. F. (SF)
Collins, T. (P)
Cone, L. (SF)
Cooper, J. (Works Manager's Office Sec)
Cox, W.
Craddock, J. (P)
Crane, M. (P)
Crawford, M. (P)
Crocker, S. (Carpenter)
Cross, K. (MF)
Crouch, B. (Auto El)
Croucher, D. (P)
Cunningham, J. A. (Trimmer)
Cunningham, J. D. (Mechanic)
Cunningham, S. (App F)
Cunningham, W. J. (F, weekend D)
Darby, W. A.
Darley, F. (P)
David, K. (P)
Davies, G. (Works Manager)
Davies, K. (P)
Davill, K.
Dawkins, S. (Fibreglass Shop)
Deacon, B. A. W (Body Works)
Delaney, P. (P)
Derby, B. (F)
Doughty, F. (Stores Foreman)
Duffy, M. (El)
Duffy, P.
Dunkley, R. (Chargehand Trimmer)
Dyson, T. (Body Shop)
Edmunds, R.
Edwards, J. (Stores Records Ck)
Eglis, E. (P)
Eyles
Farey, D. (Stores Officer)
Faulkner, C. W. (Body Shop Chargehand)
Fincher, E. (P)
Fisher, R. (P)
Fitchett, K.
Fitzhugh, S. (BB)
Flatery, L.
Ford, B. (App)
Foreman, J. (Craft Training Officer)

Freeman, P. (F)
Frisby, A. E.
Gardner, C. (Trimmer)
Gibbins, K. (Chassis Foreman)
Gibson, D. T.
Gibson, J. (CC)
Gibson, J. E. (F)
Gleave, P. K. (BB)
Glegg, K. (Chargehand)
Godbolt, J. (El)
Goldsworthy, P.
Gouldon, S. (App F)
Green, T. (F)
Griggs, J.
Gulliver, B.
Halford, K.
Hall, A. (UCE)
Hall, L. H. (CC, Stores Records Dept)
Harris, M. (Works Super)
Harrison, A. (SF)
Hawes, H. W. (Body Shop Foreman)
Haynes, S. (UCE)
Heard, G. E. T (Works Foreman)
Higton, A.
Hill, A. R.
Hill, N. O. R.
Hobbs, J.
Holmes, A. (El)
Holmes, A. H.
Horwood, B. (Works Super)
Huggett, A.
Humpreys, B. (Welder/P)
Hutchins, F.
Ingram, N.
James, B. (Stores)
James, M. (El)
Jarrold, W. (P)
Jewitt, P. (Sec)
Johnson, M. (Unit Shop Chargehand)
Johnson, S. (E Typist)
Jones, L.
Judd, M. (P)
Kalji, I. J.
Kennedy, E. (App El)
Kennedy, S. A. (App)
King, C. (Stores Records Section)
Knapton, P.
Laburnham, B. (El)
Laburnham, D. (El)
Law, W. L. (F)
Lee, C. (App)
Lee, H. A. (P)
Lloyd, M. (Works Administrator)
Lunn, S.
McAteer, H. (P)
McKail, J.
McKenzie, R. O.
Markie, J.

Marriott, C. (E Office Sec)
Mason, G. E. (SF)
Melcher, R.
Merry, D. E. (App)
Merryman, W.
Metcalfe, S. (Contract Signwriter)
Minney, F. (P)
Mitchell, M. (App)
Mitchell, R. (Works Super)
Moore, R.
Morrison, A. (Carpenter)
Moseley, D. (App)
Munday, A. (CHE)
Muscutt, R. (P)
Neale, D. (Stores Super)
Neale, K. (F)
Newton, M. (Financial Cont)
Noon, B. (Canteen Cook)
Nottage, J. E. (BM)
Ord, D. (Asst E)
Osborne, I. (Mains El)
Osbourne, T. J. (P)
Parnell, F.
Patenall, A. (App)
Percival, J. (El)
Plowman, A. (P)
Porter, L. (Trimmer)
Poulter, T. (D Trainer)
Prested, R. O.
Pullen, G. (MD, UCE)
Rappitt, C. (P)
Rattley, W. (Brake Reconditioner)
Rhodes, I. (App F)
Riches, P.
Riley, E.
Roberts, G. (Fibreglass Shop)
Rogers, B. R. (Coach P)
Rollings, B. (P)
Rowlands, P.
Ruskeys, P. E. (Pump Room Operative)
Ruskeys, P. R.
Sale, A. (P)
Sankey, J. (Chassis Shop Chargehand)
Selby, J. (P)
Shaw, P. (Trimmer)
Short, E. (P)
Slade, B. O.
Smith, B. (Body Shop)
Smith, B. (P)
Smith, C. L. (Trimmer)
Smith, G. (Pump Room Chargehand)
Smith, G. E. (Director, UCE)
Smith, G. W. (SF)
Smith, J. A. N. (Sec)
Smith, J. E.
Snedker, K. B (SF)
Stafford, B. (Body Shop

Foreman)
Stainwright, J. (Gearbox Section)
Stalkey, C. W. (Body Works)
Stanley, R. (Auto Technician)
Stenson, T. (P)
Stockley, G.
Storey, J. (App El)
Stratton, N. (P)
Tebbutt, P. (Signwriter)
Thomas, G. (SF)
Thurston, S. (Chargehand P)
Timms, L. (Coach P)
Tipler, J. W. (Mechanic)
Townsend, F. (P)
Tranter, T. (P)
Trasler, L. N. (Skilled Coach Trimmer)
Tulley, J. Jnr (SF)
Tulley, J. P. Snr (App F)
Underwood, T. (P)
Vickery, T. (Ck)
Walter, B. (P)
Walters, D. (Stationery Store Keeper)
Ward, F. (P)
Watt, G. (Director, UCE)
Watts, G.
Watts, M. (App F)
Watts, T. (Stores Lorry Driver)
Webb, T. (UCE)
Wilford, M. (Fibreglass Foreman)
Wilkins, I. (Coachbuilder)
Wilmin, N. (App)
Woolmore, T. L. (St)
Worral, M. (Trimmer)
Wright, I. (Welder)
Wright, J. (P)
Wykes, A. (Building Maintenance P)
Wykes, R. (P)
York, J. (App F)

Northampton Headquarters
Abraham, R. (Travel Sales Manager)
Adams, P. (Asst Chief E)
Appleton, J. I. (Chief DI)
Archer, G. (Traffic Office Ck)
Armstrong, H.
Baldwin, B. (Continuity Clerk)
Bandini, C. (WC)
Barden, N. (Cl)
Barker, M. (Cl)
Barltrop, R.
Barrett, J. (WC)
Bazeley, P. (WC)
Beckett, W. H. (Mechanical Inspector)

Berry, M. (Technical Asst)
Bird, J.
Birks, J. A. (TM)
Bradley, P. (TR)
Brigg, D. (TR)
Brook, J. (Purchasing Officer)
Brooke-Taylor, C. (NBC Trainee)
Brown, J. U.
Brown, K. (Accounts Manager)
Brown, M. E. (Chief Wages Clerk)
Brown, N. (CSO)
Brundle, P. (TM)
Buckby, C. (Shorthand Typist)
Buckby, J. (Asst Co Sec)
Bull, C. (D, Mobile Is' car)
Bulmer, E. (Asst Marketing Manager)
Burrows, F. (Publicity & Timetables)
Butler, H. (Marketing & Publicity Officer)
Buttifant, A. (Training Officer)
Button, S. (Trainee)
Byrine, U.
Carr, G. (Marketing Officer)
Carr, J. M. (Chief E)
Carter, A. (MD)
Carter, C. (Comptometer & Stats Record)
Cassidy, A. (Company Training Officer)
Cassidy, T. (Training Officer)
Catton, T. (Ticket Audit Section)
Chapman, D. (Ticket Audit Section)
Chapman, I. (Continuity Ck)
Chapman, J. (Express Section)
Chapman, L. A. (Chief I)
Charlton, H.
Cherry, R. (GM's Sec)
Clubb, C. (GM)
Coates, C. (Revenue Control)
Coleman, J. (WC)
Collins, M. (TR Dept)
Collins, P. (Asst TM)
Colson, B. (TM)
Connor, H. (Typist)
Cook, B. (Payroll Officer)
Costell, B. (Technical Asst)
Coward, B.
Cox, F. (Mobile I)
Cox, T. (GM, later Acting MD)
Cox, W. E. (Purchase

Ledger)
Crabbe, A. (Chief Schedules & Development Officer)
Dally, D. (TR)
Dockerill, C. (Continuity Ck)
Donnelly, A. (Revenue Control)
Dravers, E. G. (GM)
Dunkley, J. (Traffic Officer)
Dyball, K. (E Director)
Edwards, M. (Cl)
Ellay, A.
Eydman, B. (Accounts Ck)
Eyles, B. (WC)
Farrant, L. (Operations Analyst)
Faulkner, S. (TR)
Fawcett, S. (Reception/ Telephonist/Office Buyer)
Fitchett, A.
Fitchett, K. (Post Boy/ Setright E)
Flinders, W. (Office Manager)
Freeman, J. A. (MD)
Gardner, M. (TR)
Garlick, P. (Revenue Control)
Gibbons, D. (Traffic Office Ck)
Gilbert, H. (TR Officer)
Gilbert, M. (Comptometer & Stats Record)
Gillett, E. (TR)
Gingell, F. (Stores Records)
Goodman, B. (Commercial Artist)
Guest, A. (Asst TM)
Gundell, J. (Area TS, North)
Halton, M. (Canteen Liaison Officer)
Hamburg, A. F. (Vehicle Licensing Officer)
Hamilton, S. (E Director)
Hancock, S.
Hargreaves, M. I. (OM)
Harrison, D.
Hartley, J. E. (Asst TM)
Haycock, N.
Haynes, B. (TR)
Heginbotham, M. (Waybill Analysis Ck)
Herbert, B. (Instructor of Conductors)
Herbert, W. E. (Chief I)
Hiderman, T.
Hines, K. (Sales Ledger)
Hopper, A. (Payroll/ Pensions)
Horner, B. M. K. (TM)
Howcroft, B. (Express Records Ck)
Hunter, M. (Asst TM)
Jarrett, P. E. (Es' Sec)

Caple, A. E. (D?)
Carr, S. J. (D)
Cooper, J.
Cox, W. (C)
Crocket, W. (I)
Forde, P. (DAB D, I)
Franklin, W. Jnr (D)
Franklin, W. Snr (D)
Gallimore, A. S. (E)
Gray, A.
Groves, S.
Humberstone, L. W. (C)
Johnson, M. (DAB D, I)
Lang, M. (D)
Major, S. (D)
Matthews, T. D. (D, Cl)
Partridge, P. (MF)
Reader, N. (C)
Savil, W. F. (D)
Temple, B. (D)
Thorne, C. R. (D)
Townsend, A. (MF)
Warwick, R. (DS)
West, L. (D)

Thrapston
Blunt, M. (D)
Cornwall, M. (D)
George, H. (C)
Jones, B. (D)
Jones, R.
Murray, A. E. (Cs)
Procter, E. (C)
Smith, D. E. (D)
Smith, R. W. (D)

Welford
Bazeley, W. (D)
Bell, L. (C)
Davies, J. (D)
Eames, M. R. (D)
Oxley, L. (C)
Savage, L. (C)
Tait, T. G. (D)

Wellingborough
Abbott, C. (D)
Allin, J. (D)
Ames, G. (D)
Anderson, D. P. (D)
Anderson, N. (D)
Appleton, J. (D)
Atkins, P. (D)
Bailey, F. (D)
Banyard, D. (D)
Barritt, E. R. (D)
Baxter, K. A. (D)
Bedford, K. M.
Berry, M. (D)
Bolton, A.
Bolton, C.
Boot, G. S. (D)
Bradley, A. (D)
Britchford, W. L.
Broughton, A. (D)

Brown, A. (CSO)
Brown, C. E. (D)
Brown, E. (C, FC)
Brown, E. R. (D)
Brown, L. C. (D)
Brown, W. E. (D)
Browne, C. P. (I)
Butterworth, M. (D)
Button, A. (D)
Chambers, H. G. (C)
Cleary, V. F. (CSO)
Cobley, A. (TSh)
Cook, M. G. (D)
Coote, B. (S)
Cox, F. (I)
Crouch, K. C. (D)
Desai, B. (C)
Dickens, P. (I)
Dodson, P.
Donaldson, L. (D)
Dorks, A. (El)
Downes, C. (D)
Downes, G. A.
Drewe, R. E. W. (D)
Duke, P.
Dunn, M. P. (D, historian)
Edge, M. (Sec to Super)
Edgecombe, L. (DI)
Edwards, T. E. (D)
Elliott, J. (D)
Evans, H. C. (C)
Evans, R. (Tyre-fitter)
Everard, V. (Wages)
Fletcher, H. (D)
Foot, M. (C)
Garon, R. (D)
Gayton, R. C. (D)
Gibbons, K. (F)
Goulden, S. A. (D)
Goven, S. R. (D)
Greenham, R. (C)
Grimes, P. (E, North)
Grundy, W. (I)
Grundy, H. (Ck)
Gussin, T. (D)
Hall
Haseldine, H. D. (C)
Haseldine, R. A. (D)
Haynes, C. (C)
Haynes, R. (C)
Hedge, M. (D)
Hedge, P. (TSh)
Hooke, H. A. (C)
Horner, S. D. (D)
Howell, F. (F)
Howie, I. J. (D)
Hunter, J. (D)
Hutchinson, F. (D)
Inwood, W. (C)
Jones, S. (TSh Manager)
Kenyon, A. (D)
Kerrigan, J. (D)
Kilsby, R. (C)
King, C. (C)
King, D. (Chargehand)

King, L. (MF)
Knapton, P. A. (D)
Laver, A. (D)
Lewis, C. (D)
Lomley, P.
McClusky, J. (D)
MacRobert, J. (DS)
Mandalia, R. M. (D)
Marrisen, D.
Martin, J. (Cl)
May, T. (C)
Mayor, L.
Meacher, G. (F)
Messinger, J. (C)
Messinger, M. (D)
Michel, E. E. (C)
Mills, B. (S)
Minney, K. (C)
Mitchell, G. (D)
Mitchell, P.
Mobbs, M. (D)
Moore, D. (D)
Mors, B. (D)
Murtagh, T. (D)
Neville, J. (D)
O'Leary, A. J. (Csr)
Oliver, M. A. (D)
Ord, D. (Area E, North)
Ord, N. (E)
Palmer, C. (Shop Steward,
Body Works)
Palmer, S. (D)
Parker, F. W. (D)
Parnell, J. (D)
Patel, C. (C)
Perry, B.
Perry, M. (D)
Peters, F. J. (I)
Pinney, K. J. (D)
Pocock, T. (D)
Radwell, A. E. (SF)
Radwell, M.
Radwell, W. A. (C)
Rainbow, M. (D)
Riddle, S. (App F)
Robson, J. (D)
Rowell, L. (D)
Samwell, R.
Sanders, J.
Sanders, R. J. (D)
Saunders, K. J. (D)
Shadbolt, D. (S)
Sharpe, P. B. (D)
Silby, B. E. N. (Ds' Mate)
Silby, B. W. (D)
Smith, D. P. (D)
Soden, N. (D)
Spencer, G.
Spencer, S.
Spinks, M. (C)
Stewart, G. V. (D)
Summerfield, M. (D)
Tansley, J. (TSh)
Tapp, J. C. (D)
Tommaselli, A. V. (D)

Truett, G. K. (D)
Turner, S. (TSh)
Valentine, P. A. (Steam Cl)
Vandome, D. T. (D)
Waite, J. (D)
Waite, K.
Waite, T. (D)
Wallsey, J.
Waples, S. G. (D)
Warboys, D. J. (F)
Waters, C. C. R. (D)
Watson, B. J. (D)
Weatherill, L. (D)
Wedgebrow, P. (DE)
White, K. (D)
White, M. W. (D, Union
Branch Sec)
Whitney, B. (TSh)
Whitney, I.
Wignall, J. (C)
Williams, A. (C)
Willis, J. W. (F)
Winch, A. (D)
Woolsey, J. (D)
Wyatt, R. F. (Cl)

Yardley Hastings
Cox, C. (C)
Cox, S. T. (D)
Little, H. (D)
Minney, A. R. (D)
Minney, M. R. S. (Cs)
Moore, D. (D)
Parker, D. (D)
Warnes, H. W. (C)

Staff without a depot
Ambridge, W. E. (D)
Atkins, W. R. (Canteen
Asst)
Bull, W. G. A. (D)
Bultifont, A.
Burnitt, R.
Chaff, R. E. (D)
Chapman, H. G. W. (D)
Clark, B.
Farren, J. (D)
Fuller, S. J. (F)
Harrison, C.
Marrow, N. (I)
Marsh, D. (D)
Miller, J. N. (D)
Murphy, B. (D)
Neal, G. (App)
Pike, F.
Rain, M. (D)
Reeve, B. F.
Reeve, T. F.
Rodwell, W.
Senman, H.
Smith, J. H. (D)
Tebbutt, R. (P)
Waldock, R. C. (D)

Index